GCSE History is always topical with CGP...

If you're studying "Norman England, c1066–c1100" for AQA GCSE History, this CGP Topic Guide is packed with more helpful info than the Domesday Book.

It has crystal-clear notes for the whole topic, plenty of activities, sample answers, exam tips and exam-style questions. It'd be good enough to eat if the Earls weren't revolting...

How to access your free Online Edition

This book includes a free Online Edition to read on your PC, Mac or tablet. To access it, just go to **cgpbooks.co.uk/extras** and enter this code...

0855 3220 1239 1067

By the way, this code only works for one person. If somebody else has used this book before you, they might have already claimed the Online Edition.

CGP — still the best! ☺

Our sole aim here at CGP is to produce the highest quality books — carefully written, immaculately presented and dangerously close to being funny.

Then we work our socks off to get them out to you — at the cheapest possible prices.

Published by CGP

Editors: Andy Cashmore, Sophie Herring, Catherine Heygate and Jack Tooth.

With thanks to Catherine Heygate and Helen Tanner for the proofreading.
With thanks to Emily Smith for the copyright research.

Acknowledgements:
With thanks to Alamy for permission to use the image on the cover: © Hemis / Alamy Stock Photo.
With thanks to Mary Evans for permission to use the images on pages 14, 16, 22, 36 and 38.
With thanks to Look and Learn for permission to use the images on pages 21 and 57.
Image used on page 26: The Battle of Hastings, Nicolle, Pat (Patrick) (1907-95) / Private Collection / © Look and Learn / Bridgeman Images.
With thanks to Alamy for permission to use the image on page 30.
Image used on page 43: In the Days of our Forefathers, Embleton, Ron (1930-88) / Private Collection / © Look and Learn / Bridgeman Images.
Image of King Cnut and Queen Emma on page 44 from The British Library, Stowe MS 944, f.6, New Minster Liber Vitae.
Image used on page 48: © Oliver-Bonjoch. Licensed under the Creative Commons Attribution-Share Alike 2.0 Generic license.
https://creativecommons.org/licenses/by-sa/2.0/deed.en
Image used on page 59: Boy learning in Norman times, Jackson, Peter (1922-2003) / Private Collection / © Look and Learn / Bridgeman Images.

ISBN: 978 1 78908 285 2
Printed by Elanders Ltd, Newcastle upon Tyne.
Clipart from Corel®

Based on the classic CGP style created by Richard Parsons.

Contents

Exam Skills

The Normans: Conquest and Control

Life Under the Normans

The Norman Church and Monasticism

Exam Hints and Tips

GCSE AQA History is made up of <u>two papers</u>. The papers test <u>different skills</u> and each one covers <u>different topics</u>. This page gives you more information about each exam so you'll know what to expect.

You will take Two Papers altogether

Paper 1 covers the Period Study and the Wider World Depth Study

<u>Paper 1</u> is <u>2 hours</u> long. It's worth <u>84 marks</u> — <u>50%</u> of your GCSE. This paper will be divided into <u>two sections</u>:
  - Section A: <u>Period Study</u>.
  - Section B: <u>Wider World Depth Study</u>.

It's really important that you make sure you know which topics you're studying for each paper.

Paper 2 covers the Thematic Study and the British Depth Study

<u>Paper 2</u> is <u>2 hours</u> long. It's worth <u>84 marks</u> — <u>50%</u> of your GCSE. This paper will be divided into <u>two sections</u>:
  - Section A: <u>Thematic Study</u>.
  - Section B: <u>British Depth Study</u>. This also includes a question on the <u>Historic Environment</u>.

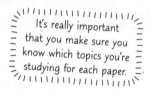

This book covers the British Depth Study <u>Norman England, c1066-c1100</u>.

Depth Studies are about knowing a Short Period in Detail

1) The depth studies cover a <u>short</u> period of history (less than 100 years) in <u>detail</u>. They focus on understanding how the <u>main features</u> and <u>events</u> of the period <u>affected</u> one another.

2) You'll need to have a detailed <u>knowledge</u> of the period — this means knowing the <u>main developments</u> and <u>important events</u> that took place. It also means understanding how <u>important features</u> of Norman England (e.g. political, social, economic and religious issues) helped to <u>shape</u> events.

3) You should know the <u>causes</u> and <u>consequences</u> of the main developments really well.

British Depth Studies include questions about Interpretations

1) <u>Interpretations</u> express <u>opinions</u> about an event or issue in the past. For example, an interpretation could be an extract from a <u>textbook</u> written by a historian or a <u>cartoon</u> drawn by a modern artist.

2) Historians and artists study <u>sources</u> when they're producing <u>interpretations</u> — sources help them to understand the past and develop their <u>point of view</u>.

3) Different historians and artists might come up with <u>different interpretations</u> of the <u>same topic</u>. There are lots of reasons why this might happen:

  - They might have used <u>different sources</u> when doing their research.
  - They may disagree over <u>how important</u> a particular source is.
  - They may have <u>different opinions</u> about how <u>significant</u> a <u>certain event</u> was.

4) For the British Depth Study part of the exam, you'll be asked to evaluate how <u>convincing</u> you think an interpretation is (see p.4 for more on this).

Exam Hints and Tips

Remember these Tips for Approaching the Questions

Stay focused on the question

- Read the questions <u>carefully</u>. Underline the <u>key words</u> in each question so you know exactly what you need to do.
- Make sure that you <u>directly answer the question</u>. Don't just chuck in everything you know about Norman England.
- You've got to be <u>relevant</u> and <u>accurate</u> — make sure you include <u>precise details</u> in your answers.
- It might help to try to write the <u>first sentence</u> of every <u>paragraph</u> in a way that <u>addresses</u> the question, e.g. "Another reason why the Harrying of the North was important was..."

> For example, you should include the <u>dates</u> of important events in the history of Norman England and the <u>names</u> of the people who were involved.

Plan your essay answers

- You <u>don't</u> need to plan answers to the <u>shorter questions</u> in the exam.
- For the <u>longer essay question</u>, it's very important to make a <u>quick plan</u> before you start writing. This will help to make your answer <u>well organised</u> and <u>structured</u>, with each point <u>leading clearly</u> to your <u>conclusion</u>.
- Look at the <u>key words</u> in the question. Scribble a <u>quick plan</u> of your <u>main points</u> — <u>cross through this neatly</u> at the end, so it's obvious it shouldn't be marked.

Organise your Time in the exam

1) Always double check that you know <u>how much time</u> you have for each paper.
2) <u>Learn the rule</u> — the <u>more marks</u> a question is worth, the <u>longer</u> your answer should be. The number of marks available for each question is clearly shown in the exam paper.
3) Try not to spend too much time on one question — you need to <u>leave enough time</u> so you can answer <u>all</u> of the questions.
4) Try to leave a few minutes at the <u>end</u> of the exam to go back and <u>read over</u> your answers.

Always use a Clear Writing Style

1) Try to use <u>clear handwriting</u> — and pay attention to <u>spelling</u>, <u>grammar</u> and <u>punctuation</u>.
2) If you make a mistake, miss out a word or need to add extra information to a point, make your changes <u>neatly</u>. Check that the examiner will still be able to <u>easily read</u> and <u>understand</u> your answer.
3) Remember to start a <u>new paragraph</u> for each new point you want to discuss.
4) A brief <u>introduction</u> and <u>conclusion</u> will help to give <u>structure</u> to your essay answers and make sure you stay <u>focused</u> on the <u>question</u>.

Learn this page and make exam stress history...

Jotting down a quick plan of the different points you're going to make before you start writing can really help you to make sure your answer is clearly written and has a nice logical structure.

Skills for the British Depth Study

This page will give you some advice on how to approach the British Depth Study, as well as how to find your way around this book. Activity types are colour-coded to help you find what you need.

The British Depth Study tests Three different Skills

The activities in this book will help you to practise all the different skills you'll need for the exam.

Knowledge and Understanding

1) You'll need to use your own knowledge and understanding of the topic to back up your answers in the exam.

2) It's important that you use accurate and relevant information to support your ideas.

> The Knowledge and Understanding activities in this book will help you to revise key features and events from the period — what was happening, when it was happening, who was involved and all the other important details.

Interpretation

1) You'll be given one interpretation about Norman England in the exam. This could be a written extract or an image.

2) You'll be asked how convincing the interpretation is in presenting an aspect of Norman England.

3) For this question, you'll need to use your own knowledge and analyse the interpretation to explain how accurate the interpretation is.

> To what extent is Interpretation 1 convincing about the Harrying of the North? Use Interpretation 1 and your own knowledge to explain your answer. [8 marks]

> The Interpretation activities in this book will help you to analyse written and visual interpretations.

Thinking Historically

1) In the exam, you'll need to use historical concepts to analyse key events and developments. These concepts include cause, consequence, change and continuity.

2) One of the questions in the exam will ask you to explain why an event or development was important in Norman England.

3) For this question, make sure you cover a range of ways the event or development affected Norman England. Make sure you explain why each effect that you cover was important.

4) Another question in the exam will ask you to write a narrative account of developments that took place between c1066 and c1100.

5) When you're answering this question, don't just describe what happened — analyse every development that you write about. Think about the impact that it had and explain how different developments were related.

> How was the feudal system important in Norman England? Explain your answer. [8 marks]

> Give an account of the ways the English Church changed after the conquest. [8 marks]

> The Thinking Historically activities in this book will help you to practise using historical concepts to analyse different parts of the topic.

Studying the Historic Environment

In the exam, you'll have to answer a 16-mark essay question about the historic environment. The next few pages are full of great advice on how to write about the Norman historic site that you've studied.

The Key Features of a Site can tell you a lot about its History

The key features of a historic site are any details, characteristics or features that stand out and make the site, or part of it, special. They are the main or most important characteristics of the site. These features can show how people lived and help to paint a picture of their culture, values and beliefs.

> Sites like castles, settlements and cathedrals can tell you a lot about how people lived in Norman England.

Use these questions to help you to identify the key features of your site...

1) How was the site used? Did this change over time?

2) Where is the site located? What was that location like?

3) Is there anything significant about the structure of the site? E.g. castles were often built with a motte and a bailey.

4) What were the key design features of the site? Think about big and small features (e.g. a monastery would normally have a cloister attached to a church, but it might also have more intricate features like stone carvings and stained glass windows).

5) Who used, designed and/or built the site? What do the site's features tell you about these people? For example, a lord's manor house might be the largest building in the village and one of the few buildings that was made of stone. This would show the lord's dominance over the village.

6) Is the site connected to any key events or developments during the period?

> For example, many castles were built to prevent rebellions by the Anglo-Saxons. However, some castles were later used as safe places to set up markets.

You can use Key Features as Evidence of Change and Continuity

1) You need to know which key features of your historic environment site changed in Norman England between c1066 and c1100.

2) Look for features that were different in an earlier period. Think about what this tells you about the way that society and culture changed in Norman England.

3) Think about what had stayed the same. These continuities might also reflect the society and culture of your site.

4) Use your knowledge of key features to support your arguments about change and continuity.

> Make sure that you understand why these features changed — consider whether the changes are linked to any major events or developments that happened in Norman England. This will help you to put the changes into context.

Historic Sites can influence Key Events and Developments

1) The nature of a historic site can influence the events and developments which happened there.

2) Understanding the key features of a site can help you to explain how and why certain events or developments happened the way they did.

> Key events like battles are often influenced by the place where they happen. The location, layout and conditions of a site can all make a difference to how an event turns out.

> In 1066, Harald Hardrada arrived at Gate Fulford with only a small part of his army. However, the Anglo-Saxons were unable to attack Hardrada's forces because the stream that divided the two armies was flooded. This meant more of Hardrada's troops were able to arrive before the battle started.

> The Anglo-Saxons couldn't attack while Hardrada's army was at its weakest. When they did attack, Hardrada's army was strong enough to win. The conditions of Gate Fulford were directly linked to the success of Hardrada's army.

Know your historic site like the back of your hand...

Don't worry if you live really far away from the historic site that you're studying — you don't need to visit the site as part of the course and you won't lose marks if you haven't been to it.

Writing About the Historic Environment

This handy page explains how to <u>choose relevant key features</u> to use as <u>evidence</u> in the exam.

Talk about Relevant Key Features in the Exam

In the exam, you'll be asked about the <u>site</u> that you've studied. You'll need to use your <u>own knowledge</u> of the <u>key features</u> of your site to <u>answer</u> an essay question. In your <u>essay</u>, you'll be asked to link the <u>historic environment</u> (your site) to an <u>aspect</u> of Norman England that you've looked at in your <u>depth study</u>.

1) The question might focus on a <u>key change</u> or <u>period of continuity</u>, or it could ask you to examine the <u>causes</u> or <u>consequences</u> of an <u>event</u> or <u>development</u>.

2) Only talk about <u>features</u> of your site that are <u>relevant</u> to the <u>question</u> that you've been asked and to the <u>points</u> that you're making in your answer.

3) You need to <u>select</u> pieces of information that <u>support</u> your arguments.

See p.7 for some <u>examples</u> of how to use key features in your answer.

Different Features can tell you Different Things

When you're talking about <u>key features</u>, you could choose something quite <u>broad</u>, like the <u>physical location</u> of the site, or focus on <u>very small details</u>, like a <u>specific type of decoration</u> in a building.

1) Think about the <u>location</u> of your site and what was <u>around it</u>. There's often a reason <u>why</u> a certain place was chosen (e.g. it was easy to defend), and this can <u>reveal</u> things about the <u>lives</u> of those who used the site.

2) Consider how a site is <u>used over time</u> — changes in <u>function</u> can reflect <u>gradual changes</u> in society, or be a result of <u>upheaval</u> or a significant <u>event</u>.

3) <u>Design</u> features often reflect <u>key attitudes</u> or <u>changes</u> in the owners' lives.

4) They can also tell you a lot about the <u>motives</u> of the people who <u>used</u> or <u>created</u> the site. Think about the <u>physical structure</u> of your site and what it tells you about the way it was <u>used</u> and the people who <u>designed</u> it.

For example, a <u>wooden castle</u> might have been strengthened with <u>stone walls</u>. This might suggest that the <u>owner</u> was concerned about <u>maintaining control</u> of the local area and wanted to make the castle's <u>defences stronger</u> in case it was <u>attacked</u>.

5) Pick out features that are <u>representative</u> of Norman England. Some features might be <u>unique</u> to your site, while others might be <u>typical</u> of Norman England and pop up in lots of sites.

Use your Own Knowledge to put Key Features into Context

1) Use what you know about <u>Norman England</u> to put the key features of your site into <u>context</u>.

2) Talk about your site's <u>development</u> in the context of <u>wider changes</u> or <u>events</u> in Norman England.

3) For example, design choices often reflect <u>wider cultural changes</u> — <u>fashions</u> change over time and key features can be used as <u>evidence</u> of <u>how</u> and <u>when</u> these changes affected a <u>particular site</u>.

4) When you identify a <u>feature</u>, talk about what it might <u>suggest</u> about the people who used the site, then <u>link</u> it to <u>wider developments</u>.

For example, new design features like <u>high arches</u> and <u>large stone pillars</u> might have been used in a <u>cathedral</u> — this could suggest that the people who built the cathedral had been influenced by the <u>Romanesque style of architecture</u>, which was popular in <u>Normandy</u> and much of <u>Western Europe</u>.

The Normans <u>popularised</u> the use of <u>Romanesque architecture</u> in England, where it was uncommon before 1066. <u>Design features</u> can be <u>evidence</u> of this <u>change in architectural style</u> — they can indicate that the building was constructed by <u>Normans</u> after 1066 rather than by <u>Anglo-Saxons</u> before the conquest.

Writing About the Historic Environment

You'll need to use your Knowledge of Key Features in the Exam

You'll get one question in the exam about your historic site. It'll look a bit like this:

The question starts by making a statement that's linked to a particular type of site (e.g. castles).

'The main purpose of Norman castles was to allow the Normans to gain and maintain control of England.'

To what extent does a study of Pevensey Castle support this statement?

Explain your answer, referring to Pevensey Castle and your knowledge of Norman England. [16 marks]

The question will name a specific site (in the exam, it'll be the one that you've studied).

You'll need to use evidence from your site to answer the question. Always support your points by drawing on your knowledge of your site's key features.

Use the Key Features of your site to Support your Answer

Select key features that are relevant to the question and use them to support your points. Explain how the key features of your site support (or go against) the statement in the question.

As one of the first Norman castles built in England, Pevensey Castle was crucial to the Normans gaining control in the early days of the conquest. The castle was built as a temporary defence when the Normans first landed in England in September 1066, constructed within an old Roman fort using timber that had been brought over from Normandy. Building the castle out of wood rather than stone and using elements of the existing Roman structure allowed the Normans to build the castle quickly. The swift construction of Pevensey Castle helped the Normans to establish a foothold in England.

The development of Pevensey Castle's defences shows that castles were used to maintain control after William I became King of England. In 1067, William gave Pevensey to his half-brother, Robert, Count of Mortain, who refortified the castle. Robert repaired the walls of the Roman fort and created an inner bailey and an outer bailey, separated by a ditch and a wooden palisade. These features, which strengthened the castle's defences, were also used in many other Norman castles at the time. The strong defences of castles allowed the Normans to secure their lands and to repel Anglo-Saxon attacks, helping them to maintain control of England.

You can use the actions or motives of people who were linked to your site to support your arguments. Try to link their actions to events in wider society.

You can also use your knowledge of the period to support your arguments and link your site to wider developments. Don't just write down everything you know about the period — you need to answer the question.

The location of Pevensey Castle was important in helping the Normans gain and maintain control of England. Pevensey is located on the south coast, giving access to the English Channel and the route between Normandy and England. Securing this route was crucial because William was Duke of Normandy as well as King of England and spent a lot of time in Normandy, and many of his lords also held lands in both territories. Pevensey Castle therefore indicates that castles helped to maintain control of England by defending strategically important locations.

Key features — small, metal, good at opening doors...

There are different types of historic sites you might study — yours might be a specific building like a church, or it might cover a larger area like a town or the site of a revolt or a battle.

Exam Skills

King Edward and the Godwins

Edward the Confessor was King of England from 1042 to 1066, but he didn't have complete authority — people like Godwin, Earl of Wessex, and his children had a say in the running of the kingdom too.

Edward the Confessor stabilised England

1) Edward's father was Aethelred II, an Anglo-Saxon who was King of England from 978. However, the Scandinavians invaded England in 1013, and took control of the kingdom after a period of upheaval.

2) After the invasion, Edward fled to Normandy. He remained in exile for over twenty years. Between 1013 and 1042, England's kings included three Scandinavians — Swein, Cnut and Harthacnut.

3) When Harthacnut died in 1042, Edward returned to England and became king. Many powerful figures were still loyal to the old Scandinavian rulers, so Edward had to assert his own authority:

- Godwin of Wessex, Siward of Northumbria and Leofric of Mercia were the most powerful earls (see p.28) in England. Edward acted quickly to gain their support.
- Edward had to defend against foreign claimants to the throne, such as King Magnus of Norway. He prepared for an invasion by maintaining a fleet on the south coast, but Magnus never came.
- Edward gave important positions in the royal household and the Church to the followers he had gained in Normandy — many Anglo-Saxons, including Godwin, resented this foreign influence.

The Godwins Dominated English Politics

1) Godwin had been the Earl of Wessex since 1018 — it was the oldest and richest earldom in the whole kingdom. In 1042, Godwin supported Edward's claim to the throne and a few years later Edward married Godwin's daughter (Edith). This gave Godwin even more power and influence.

2) However, Godwin became less powerful as the king started to favour the Normans in the royal household. In 1051, Godwin rebelled unsuccessfully against Edward and was sent into exile.

> Edward ordered Godwin to punish the town of Dover after a fight between the townspeople and a visiting French noble — Godwin refused. He gathered an army and went to confront the king, but didn't have enough men to overpower the king's forces.

3) In 1052, Godwin returned to England with an army. The king didn't want to fight Godwin, so restored him as Earl of Wessex.

4) Godwin's son, Harold, was Earl of East Anglia. When Godwin died in 1053, Harold gave up East Anglia to be Earl of Wessex. He was now the most powerful man in England after the king.

5) Harold played an important role in governing the country. Edward knew he couldn't rule without the support of the nobility, so had to work with earls like Harold. As the king got older, Harold was more and more responsible for helping to run the kingdom.

6) Harold and his siblings were dominant figures in England in the final years of Edward's reign. His brothers (Tostig, Gyrth and Leofwine) were also earls, and his sister (Edith) was the queen.

> The Godwins controlled a huge amount of land across the kingdom. These lands made the Godwins very wealthy, helping them to acquire a large number of followers. They gained support by giving land and other gifts to their allies, and paid skilled fighters to join their households.

England faced a Succession Crisis when King Edward Died

1) Edward died in January 1066. He didn't have any children, so there was no clear successor to the throne.

2) Due to the close connections between England, Normandy and Scandinavia (see above), there were people in all three regions who believed they had a strong claim to the throne.

3) When an Anglo-Saxon king died, the Witan could play a role in choosing the successor, especially if there was a dispute over who should rule. They knew foreign threats were likely, so needed to choose a strong leader to protect the country.

> The Witan was the king's council — a group of powerful lords and high-ranking churchmen who advised the king and helped him govern.

King Edward and the Godwins

SKILLS PRACTICE

There's a lot of background information on the previous page about King Edward and his relationship with the Godwins. Make sure you know all about Edward and the Godwins with the activities on this page.

Knowledge and Understanding

1) Explain who each of the following people was:
   a) Edward
   b) Harthacnut
   c) Godwin
   d) Harold
   e) Edith
   f) Tostig, Gyrth and Leofwine

2) Copy and complete the timeline below by filling in the key events for Edward and the Godwin family that happened in each year. Try to give as much detail as you can.

3) Give three ways that Edward asserted his authority after becoming king.

4) Using the key words below, explain why the Godwins were powerful in Anglo-Saxon England. Give as much information as possible.

   wealth   land   military strength

Thinking Historically

1) 'King Edward had a lot of power over the Godwins.'
   a) Write a paragraph agreeing with the statement above.
   b) Write a paragraph disagreeing with the statement above.
   c) Write a conclusion summarising how far you agree with the statement above.

2) Using the key words below, explain why there was a succession crisis in England in 1066.

   children   Normandy   Scandinavia

EXAM TIP

Edward the Confessor was up to the earls in Godwins...

When you're studying the Norman Conquest, you need to know about the events that led up to it and why they happened. This includes the succession crisis that came after Edward's death.

The Normans: Conquest and Control

Claimants to the Throne in 1066

When King Edward died in 1066, there were a few different people who all had a claim to the empty throne.

There were Two Englishmen with a Claim to the Throne

1) At the start of 1066, Edgar Atheling and Harold Godwinson were both in a position to inherit the throne. However, Harold was in a much stronger position than Edgar.

2) Edgar Atheling was a relative of King Edward. However, Edgar was only a teenager and he hadn't proven himself as a leader, which made it difficult for him to gain support from the Witan (see p.8).

Comment and Analysis

There were no fixed rules about succession, but being related to the king could strengthen someone's claim. However, even those with a strong claim had to be able to use military force to take control of the country and show they would be an effective ruler.

3) Harold was the most powerful nobleman in England and he had experience of leading an army. He was close to the royal family — his father helped Edward to become king, and his sister was Edward's wife (see p.8). Harold claimed Edward had asked him to become king on his deathbed.

4) Harold was ambitious and thought that becoming king might secure his authority. In the past, powerful earls had been seen as a threat to royal authority, so a new king might have tried to reduce Harold's power in England. Harold could prevent this from happening by taking the throne.

> Harold's brother, Tostig, had also been a powerful nobleman, but he had been exiled in 1065. Tostig was Earl of Northumbria, but was unpopular with the Northumbrians, and they rebelled against him. King Edward sent Harold to deal with the rebels, but instead Harold agreed to send Tostig into exile and to appoint a new earl (Morcar). Tostig's exile removed one of Harold's potential rivals for the throne.

William of Normandy thought he was the Rightful Successor

1) William was the Duke of Normandy. He was a powerful and successful military leader with many years of experience. He had defeated several challenges to his leadership and brought stability to Normandy.

2) William was related to King Edward, and claimed Edward had sent Harold to Normandy to promise him the throne. Harold definitely went to Normandy in 1064 or 1065, but it's unclear what really happened:

- According to Norman sources, Harold had been sent by King Edward to name William as the next King of England — Harold supposedly swore an oath to support William's claim.
- According to some English sources, Harold went to secure the release of his brother and his nephew, who had been hostages in Normandy since 1051. However, others suggest Harold was shipwrecked on the northern coast of France during a fishing trip.
- In the English sources, Harold still swore the oath to support William's claim, but it wasn't the reason for visiting Normandy — some of them argue that William forced him to do it.

3) William's claim was also supported by the Pope (see p.50), emphasising that God was on his side.

4) Becoming King of England would make William more powerful. As Duke of Normandy, he was meant to serve the King of France — if he took the throne, he would have the same high status as the French king.

Harald Hardrada wanted to Conquer England

1) Harald Hardrada was the King of Norway. He was another experienced ruler who was known for his military prowess. He claimed he was the true successor to the Scandinavian kings who had ruled England before Edward the Confessor.

> Hardrada wanted to reconquer the empire of King Cnut, who had ruled over Norway, Denmark and England earlier in the 11th century.

2) His claim was supported by Harold Godwinson's brother, Tostig, who had already tried to make allies in France and Scotland since his exile. By supporting Hardrada, Tostig might have hoped to get revenge on his brother and reclaim his former earldom of Northumbria.

Claimants to the Throne in 1066

When you're writing about the events of 1066, there are lots of important names to get your head around. The activities on this page take a look at the most important figures in the struggle to become King of England.

Knowledge and Understanding

1) For each of the following claimants to the throne in 1066, explain who they were and why they wanted to be King of England.

    a) Harold Godwinson   b) William of Normandy   c) Harald Hardrada

2) In Anglo-Saxon England, there were no fixed rules about who would succeed to the throne when a king died. What factors were important in deciding who would be the next king?

3) Copy and complete the table below, explaining what information the Norman and English sources give about Harold's visit to Normandy.

Norman Sources	English Sources

Thinking Historically

1) Copy and complete the table below, explaining what you think the strengths and weaknesses of each person's claim to the throne were in 1066. Try to give as much detail as possible.

Claimant	Strengths	Weaknesses
a) Edgar Atheling		
b) Harold Godwinson		
c) William of Normandy		
d) Harald Hardrada		

2) Who do you think had the strongest claim to the throne in 1066? Explain your answer.

Use your table from question 1 to help you answer questions 2 and 3.

3) Explain who you think had the weakest claim to the throne in 1066.

An Englishman, a Norman and a Viking went into a war...

There's a lot of key information to learn about 1066 — make sure you know the order that events happened in, the names of all the important figures and the roles these people played.

The Struggle for the Throne

The Witan chose Harold Godwinson as the next King of England, and he was crowned on the same day as Edward was buried. Unfortunately for Harold, his rival claimants weren't willing to give up without a fight.

Harold was Prepared for an invasion in Mid-1066

1) Once Harold had been crowned king, he gathered his forces and prepared to defend the south coast in case the Normans invaded. Harold's army consisted of housecarls, who were well-trained professional warriors, and the fyrd, a part-time defensive force.

> The fyrd was made up of ordinary men who had to leave their normal work and provide military service whenever the king summoned them. Members of the fyrd weren't professional fighters and they usually only served for two months at a time.

2) The Anglo-Saxons waited on the south coast throughout mid-1066, but nothing happened. By September, supplies were running low and Harold's men needed to return to their land to collect the harvest, so he dismissed the fyrd and returned to London.

Harold Defeated the Scandinavian Invaders...

1) After Harold dismissed the fyrd, an army led by Harald Hardrada and supported by Tostig (see p.10) invaded north-eastern England.

2) On 20th September, Hardrada defeated Harold's allies, Earl Edwin of Mercia and Earl Morcar of Northumbria, at the Battle of Gate Fulford.

> Edwin and Morcar were younger and less knowledgeable than Hardrada, who was very experienced in battle. The Scandinavians were fierce and skilled fighters compared to the less experienced Anglo-Saxons.

3) Harold went north to face Hardrada. He had dismissed the fyrd, so he had to gather troops on the way. However, Harold arrived in the north quickly.

4) Hardrada had asked for hostages from the Anglo-Saxons after his victory at Gate Fulford, and went to Stamford Bridge to collect them. He wasn't expecting a battle, so he didn't take his whole army.

5) Harold took Hardrada by surprise. This gave him an advantage, and he defeated the invaders at the Battle of Stamford Bridge on 25th September. Hardrada and Tostig were both killed, along with huge numbers of their men. The remains of the Scandinavian army withdrew from England.

... but he was Defeated by the Normans at the Battle of Hastings

1) The Normans landed near Pevensey on 28th September and started pillaging (raiding and stealing from) Harold's lands. This forced Harold to hurry south to defend his people and try to drive the Normans out.

2) Harold spent a few days in London, but he didn't have time to gather all his troops, or to recover from the long march and the Battle of Stamford Bridge.

3) On 14th October 1066, the Anglo-Saxon and Norman armies faced each other at the Battle of Hastings.

4) Harold chose a strong defensive position for his army — the top of a ridge. This suited the Anglo-Saxon tactic of using the housecarls' shields to make a defensive wall in front of the army. This tactic worked at first, and the Normans couldn't break through. However, the Normans eventually broke the shield wall:

- Part of the Norman army used a tactic called feigned flight — they pretended to run away. Some of the Anglo-Saxon army left their position to follow them.

- This weakened the Anglo-Saxons' defences, as the shield wall relied on everyone holding their position in the line. Once the shield wall was broken, the Norman cavalry (horsemen) could ride through and kill many of the Anglo-Saxon fighters.

- Harold was killed (possibly by a Norman arrow) — his brothers and allies Gyrth and Leofwine were also killed in the battle. The Anglo-Saxon army was defeated.

The Struggle for the Throne

The battles at Gate Fulford, Stamford Bridge and Hastings were hugely important events in Harold's short reign. These activities will get you thinking about the impact of the battles in more detail.

Knowledge and Understanding

1) Write a definition for each of the following terms:

a) Fyrd

b) Housecarl

2) Harold was only King of England for nine months, but a lot of important events took place during his reign. Copy and complete the timeline below by filling in the events that happened at each point. Try to give as much detail as possible.

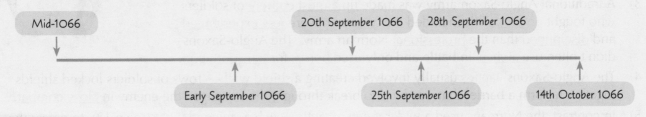

Mid-1066   20th September 1066   28th September 1066

Early September 1066   25th September 1066   14th October 1066

Thinking Historically

1) Copy and complete the table below, stating whether the Anglo-Saxons won or lost each battle and explaining why this was the outcome. Give as much detail as possible.

Battle	Did the Anglo-Saxons win or lose?	Explanation for outcome
a) Gate Fulford		
b) Stamford Bridge		

2) Copy and complete the mind map below, explaining how the following factors influenced the outcome of the Battle of Hastings.

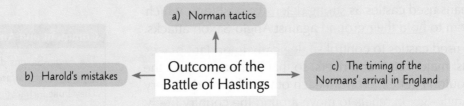

a) Norman tactics

b) Harold's mistakes ← Outcome of the Battle of Hastings → c) The timing of the Normans' arrival in England

I'm quivering at the idea of getting shot with an arrow...

In the exam, it's worth taking a moment to plan out your answer before you start writing. This will help you to make sure that each of the points you make is answering the question.

The Normans: Conquest and Control

Norman Military Tactics

The Anglo-Saxons and the Normans had different ideas on <u>military tactics</u>. In 1066, the Normans brought <u>military innovations</u> to England that the Anglo-Saxons didn't know much about, such as <u>cavalry</u> and <u>castles</u>.

The Normans and Anglo-Saxons Fought in Different Ways

© Mary Evans Picture Library

1) The Norman army was <u>strong</u> and <u>well equipped</u>. It included a mixture of <u>foot-soldiers</u>, <u>archers</u> and <u>cavalry</u>. The archers were especially <u>effective</u> at the Battle of Hastings. They were able to attack from a <u>distance</u>, meaning they could <u>weaken</u> the Anglo-Saxon <u>shield wall</u> without <u>risking their lives</u>.

2) The cavalry was also an important part of the Norman army. The riders were <u>highly skilled</u> and <u>disciplined</u>, and fighting on <u>horseback</u> allowed them to attack with <u>greater speed</u> and <u>strength</u>. This might have helped the Normans to <u>break through</u> the Anglo-Saxon <u>shield wall</u> at Hastings.

3) A traditional Anglo-Saxon army was made up <u>almost entirely</u> of soldiers who fought <u>on foot</u>. This included the <u>fyrd</u>, who were <u>less experienced</u> and <u>disciplined</u> than the <u>professional</u> Norman army. The Anglo-Saxons didn't often use <u>archers</u> in battle and only used <u>horses</u> for <u>transportation</u>.

4) The Anglo-Saxons' <u>tactics</u> usually involved creating a <u>shield wall</u> — rows of soldiers locked shields together to form a barrier that was hard to break through, then engaged the enemy in <u>close combat</u>.

5) In contrast, the Normans used a <u>wider range of tactics</u>, such as <u>feigned flight</u> (see p.12), to defeat the enemy. They were also more experienced than the Anglo-Saxons at <u>attacking</u> and <u>defending castles</u>.

The Normans built Castles throughout England

1) When the Normans landed at <u>Pevensey</u> in 1066, they immediately started building a <u>castle</u> — they also built one at <u>Hastings</u> before the battle there. This allowed William to fight from a <u>strong base</u>.

2) After William won at Hastings, he built castles <u>all over England</u>:

- Some castles were built to <u>prevent invasion</u>. Castles along the <u>south coast</u> (e.g. Dover, Arundel, Corfe) helped to protect England from an invasion <u>by sea</u>, while castles along the border with <u>Wales</u> (e.g. Chester, Shrewsbury, Hereford) were built to prevent a <u>Welsh</u> invasion.

- Castles were often built as a <u>response</u> to Anglo-Saxon <u>rebellions</u>. For example, William built a castle in <u>Exeter</u> after defeating an <u>uprising</u> in the town in 1068.

- Castles were also a <u>highly visible symbol</u> of the Normans' <u>dominance</u> and <u>control</u> over England.

Castles were a Key Part of the Normans' Military Strategy

1) The Normans used castles as <u>strong defensive positions</u>, which helped them to <u>hold their ground</u> against Anglo-Saxon attacks.

2) They also used castles to control <u>strategically important places</u> (e.g. towns, major roads and rivers) so that Normans across the country couldn't get <u>cut off</u> from each other. This made it very hard for <u>Anglo-Saxon rebels</u> to <u>move around</u> the country <u>freely</u>.

3) The network of castles <u>throughout England</u> meant that William could station Norman soldiers <u>all over the country</u>. This meant that soldiers could be <u>sent quickly</u> to deal with <u>local rebellions</u>.

4) Castles weren't just defensive — they were also used as <u>bases</u> so Norman troops could launch <u>attacks</u> on the surrounding <u>territory</u>. This helped the Normans to bring more <u>land</u> under their <u>control</u>.

Comment and Analysis

The Anglo-Saxons didn't have a lot of <u>experience</u> of warfare involving <u>castles</u>. They built <u>fortifications</u> before 1066, using simple features such as <u>ditches</u>, <u>earth banks</u> and <u>fences</u>, but these were significantly <u>less advanced</u> than <u>motte and bailey castles</u> (see p.16). This gave the Normans a big <u>military advantage</u> over the Anglo-Saxons who rebelled against their rule after 1066.

Norman Military Tactics

The Normans' military innovations helped them to gain control of England — try the activities below to see if you know what these innovations were and how they made the conquest easier for the Normans.

Thinking Historically

1) Copy and complete the table below, listing the similarities and differences between the Anglo-Saxon army and the Norman army at the Battle of Hastings. Use the information on pages 12 and 14 to help you. Give as much detail as possible.

Similarities	Differences

Knowledge and Understanding

1) Copy and complete the table below, giving as much detail as possible about why the following castles were built.

Castles	Why they were built
a) Pevensey, Hastings	
b) Dover, Arundel, Corfe	
c) Chester, Shrewsbury, Hereford	
d) Exeter	

2) Explain why the Normans' use of castles put the Anglo-Saxons at a military disadvantage.

3) Copy and complete the mind map below, giving the different ways that castles were used as part of the Normans' military strategy.

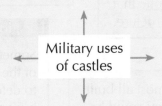

Military uses of castles

Maybe William just appreciated a nice castle...

In the exam, you'll need to use correct terminology (e.g. the fyrd) in your answer. This is a good way of showing the examiner that you really understand the topic you're writing about.

The Design of Norman Castles

Norman castles were designed to combine <u>military strength</u> with <u>living accommodation</u>.
They had to be <u>easy to defend</u>, but also <u>practical</u> for people to <u>live</u> and <u>work</u> inside them.

Most Norman Castles in England were Motte and Bailey Castles

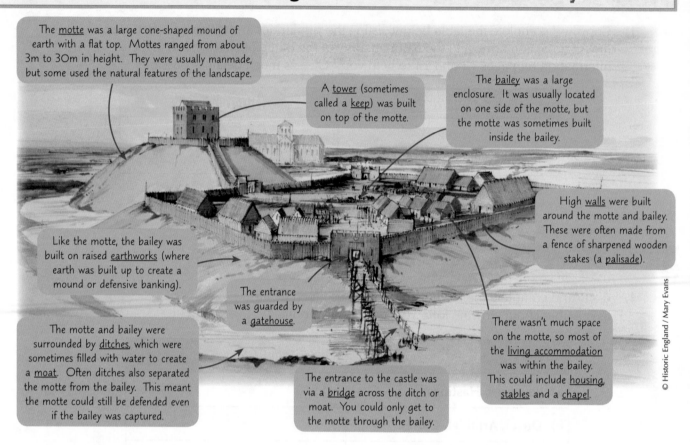

The <u>motte</u> was a large cone-shaped mound of earth with a flat top. Mottes ranged from about 3m to 30m in height. They were usually manmade, but some used the natural features of the landscape.

A <u>tower</u> (sometimes called a <u>keep</u>) was built on top of the motte.

The <u>bailey</u> was a large enclosure. It was usually located on one side of the motte, but the motte was sometimes built inside the bailey.

High <u>walls</u> were built around the motte and bailey. These were often made from a fence of sharpened wooden stakes (a <u>palisade</u>).

Like the motte, the bailey was built on raised <u>earthworks</u> (where earth was built up to create a mound or defensive banking).

The entrance was guarded by a <u>gatehouse</u>.

The motte and bailey were surrounded by <u>ditches</u>, which were sometimes filled with water to create a <u>moat</u>. Often ditches also separated the motte from the bailey. This meant the motte could still be defended even if the bailey was captured.

The entrance to the castle was via a <u>bridge</u> across the ditch or moat. You could only get to the motte through the bailey.

There wasn't much space on the motte, so most of the <u>living accommodation</u> was within the bailey. This could include <u>housing</u>, <u>stables</u> and a <u>chapel</u>.

© Historic England / Mary Evans

Castles Weren't all the Same

Although the motte and bailey design was very common, Norman castles <u>varied</u> in <u>size</u>, <u>structure</u>, <u>building materials</u> and <u>location</u>.

Size

Some Norman castles were <u>large</u> and <u>complex</u>. However, many others were <u>small</u> and <u>simple</u> — they just had a <u>low motte</u> that was topped with a <u>simple wooden structure</u>.

Structure

Norman castles <u>didn't all</u> use the <u>motte and bailey</u> design. For example, <u>Exeter Castle</u> didn't have a <u>motte</u> or <u>keep</u> — it was just a <u>fortified enclosure</u>.

Building Materials

The earliest Norman castles were almost all built from <u>wood</u> and <u>earth</u>. This meant they could be built <u>quickly</u> and <u>without skilled labour</u>. Lots of <u>wooden</u> castles were <u>replaced</u> with <u>stone</u> castles later on. For example, in <u>1070</u>, William ordered that <u>Hastings Castle</u> should be rebuilt using stone.

Location

Sometimes, the Normans used <u>natural</u> parts of the <u>landscape</u> to make their castles easier to defend. For example, <u>Richmond Castle</u> was built next to a <u>steep drop</u> into the River Swale. They also reused existing <u>Anglo-Saxon structures</u>. The castles at <u>Pevensey</u> and <u>Exeter</u> were built inside <u>fortifications</u> that had existed <u>before</u> the conquest.

The Design of Norman Castles

There are lots of key words and design features related to motte and bailey castles — use these activities to check whether you understand all of the different features of a castle and know what their purpose was.

Knowledge and Understanding

1) Explain what is meant by the following terms:

   a) Motte   b) Bailey   c) Keep

2) Why were the earliest Norman castles built from wood?

3) Not all Norman castles were built in the same way. For each of the following castles, describe one unusual feature of the way it was built.
   a) Richmond
   b) Exeter
   c) Pevensey

Thinking Historically

1) The diagram below shows a plan of how a motte and bailey castle might look if it was viewed from above. Describe each labelled feature and explain why it was important. Give as much detail as possible.

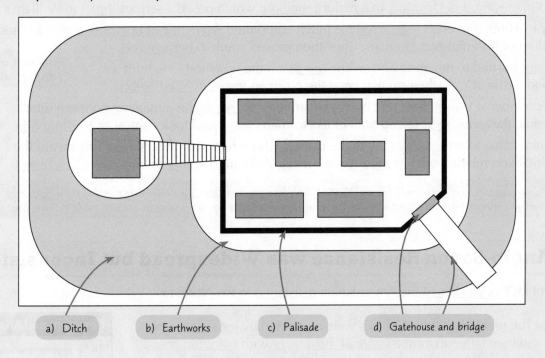

a) Ditch   b) Earthworks   c) Palisade   d) Gatehouse and bridge

Make sure you know your motte from your moat...

It's important to be able to describe key features of castles, but you also need to understand the reasons why the Normans built castles and how they helped William to gain control of England.

Resistance to Norman Rule, 1067-1069

William became <u>King of England</u> on <u>25th December 1066</u>, but the Anglo-Saxons weren't happy about it. For William, the hard work of getting the kingdom <u>under control</u> was only just starting...

There were Constant Rebellions all over the Kingdom

1067
- Anglo-Saxon rebels launched an <u>unsuccessful attack</u> on <u>Dover Castle</u> in Kent. They were helped by <u>Eustace II of Boulogne</u>, a French noble who may have wanted to take control of Dover for himself.
- The Anglo-Saxon thegn (see p.28) <u>Eadric the Wild</u>, whose lands had been <u>seized</u> by the Normans, attacked <u>Hereford Castle</u> (near Wales).

1068
- There was a revolt in <u>Exeter</u>, probably in response to <u>tax increases</u>. At the same time, <u>Harold Godwinson's sons</u> raided the <u>south west</u> by sea.
- <u>Edwin</u> and <u>Morcar</u> (see p.12) launched a rebellion in <u>Mercia</u> with support from the <u>Welsh</u>. There was also unrest in <u>Northumbria</u>.

> Edwin was still <u>Earl of Mercia</u> in 1068, but the appointment of other earls by William had <u>limited his authority</u>. Morcar had been <u>replaced</u> as <u>Earl of Northumbria</u> in around 1067.

William and his supporters successfully <u>put down</u> these rebellions using <u>military force</u> and the <u>construction of castles</u> (see p.14). William treated the rebels who <u>surrendered</u> to him <u>leniently</u>. For example, when <u>Exeter</u> surrendered, he promised to <u>protect</u> the town's inhabitants. He was also lenient to <u>Edwin</u> and <u>Morcar</u>, granting them their <u>lives</u> and their <u>freedom</u>.

There was a Major Revolt in Northern England in 1069

1) In <u>1069</u>, a group of northern nobles joined forces with <u>Edgar Atheling</u>, <u>King Malcolm III of Scotland</u> and <u>King Swein II of Denmark</u> in a major <u>rebellion</u>, which posed a serious <u>threat</u> to William's rule.

2) Early in 1069, the rebels <u>massacred</u> the newly-appointed <u>Norman Earl of Northumbria</u> and several hundred of his knights at <u>Durham</u>. They then moved south to <u>besiege York</u>.

3) <u>William</u> hurried to the north and swiftly <u>put down</u> the rebellion. He built a second castle at <u>York</u>, then strengthened the Norman forces in <u>Northumbria</u>.

For more on the response to this rebellion, see p.20.

4) In September, a <u>Danish</u> fleet sent by Swein arrived and <u>joined</u> the remaining northern rebels. Together, they took <u>York</u>, seized both of its Norman <u>castles</u> and took control of <u>Northumbria</u>.

5) William came to an <u>agreement</u> with the Danes, who returned to their ships. This meant the Anglo-Saxon rebels were <u>unsupported</u>, allowing William to <u>scatter</u> them and <u>regain control</u>.

> There was <u>unrest</u> in other places — Eadric the Wild and the Welsh attacked <u>Shrewsbury</u>, there were risings in the <u>west country</u>, and Edwin and Morcar led another rebellion in <u>Mercia</u>. William's local forces dealt with the unrest in the <u>south</u> and <u>west</u>, while William marched to the <u>north</u>.

The Anglo-Saxon Resistance was Widespread but Inconsistent

A range of factors <u>weakened</u> the Anglo-Saxon <u>resistance</u> to the Normans:

- The rebels in different places were motivated by <u>local concerns</u>, so they <u>failed</u> to form a <u>national movement</u> with <u>common goals</u>.
- There was no <u>single</u>, <u>strong leader</u> who <u>all</u> the rebels supported.
- The rebels <u>didn't</u> have a <u>shared strategy</u> and they failed to <u>coordinate</u> their uprisings, making it <u>easier to defeat</u> them.
- Many English nobles actually <u>supported</u> William and some even <u>helped</u> him to <u>fight</u> the <u>rebels</u>. Others just <u>didn't take sides</u> at all.

Comment and Analysis

These problems would eventually make resisting the Normans seem <u>hopeless</u>. Many rebels were <u>killed</u> or forced into <u>exile</u>, and those who remained in England may have gradually started to <u>accept</u> that the Normans had come to stay.

Resistance to Norman Rule, 1067-1069

SKILLS PRACTICE

There were lots of rebellions against the Normans after William became king. These activities will make sure you know the details of all of these rebellions and how William responded to them.

Knowledge and Understanding

1) Give as much detail as possible about the rebellions that happened in each of these places in the given year:
   a) Dover Castle, 1067
   b) Hereford Castle, 1067
   c) Exeter, 1068
   d) South-west England, 1068
   e) Mercia, 1068

2) The flowchart below shows the key events that took place during the northern rebellion in 1069. Copy and complete the flowchart by adding the missing events.

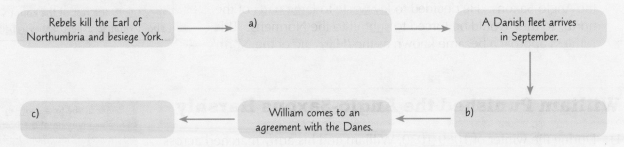

Rebels kill the Earl of Northumbria and besiege York. → a) → A Danish fleet arrives in September.

c) ← William comes to an agreement with the Danes. ← b)

3) Give four reasons why the Anglo-Saxon resistance to the Normans was ineffective.

Interpretation

The interpretation below is about Anglo-Saxon resistance to Norman rule.

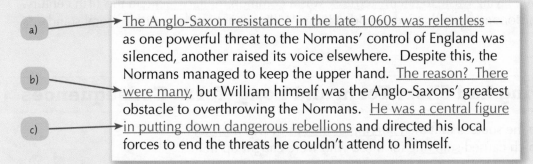

a) The Anglo-Saxon resistance in the late 1060s was relentless — as one powerful threat to the Normans' control of England was silenced, another raised its voice elsewhere. Despite this, the Normans managed to keep the upper hand. b) The reason? There were many, but William himself was the Anglo-Saxons' greatest obstacle to overthrowing the Normans. c) He was a central figure in putting down dangerous rebellions and directed his local forces to end the threats he couldn't attend to himself.

1) Explain whether you find each of the highlighted phrases above convincing about Anglo-Saxon resistance to the Normans.

EXAM TIP

William made more enemies after he became king...

When you're writing about an interpretation, look at the interpretation carefully to make sure you understand the point it's making. Highlighting key features or quotes can help you do this.

The Harrying of the North

William's response to the revolt in 1069 was <u>merciless</u>, but <u>effective</u>. It put an end to <u>resistance</u> in the <u>north</u> and <u>cemented his authority</u> as king, just when he was starting to feel the pressure...

The 1069 Revolt led to the Harrying of the North

1) William tried to keep as many <u>Anglo-Saxons</u> on his side as he could after the conquest. However, the <u>northern revolt</u> in <u>1069</u> showed that William's approach <u>wasn't working</u>.

2) The northern revolt was an <u>unprecedented</u> threat to William's authority, because the rebels in the north were also <u>supported</u> by <u>powerful foreign forces</u>, including the <u>Scots</u> and the <u>Danes</u>.

3) William was facing <u>other rebellions</u> all over the country at the time. This meant that he needed to <u>act quickly</u> and <u>decisively</u>.

4) These developments forced William to change his approach to the Anglo-Saxons. He decided to <u>lay waste</u> to <u>large parts</u> of the north, so they would be forced to <u>submit</u> to the Normans. This <u>ruthless approach</u> became known as the '<u>Harrying of the North</u>'.

Comment and Analysis

William's goal was to <u>avoid</u> any <u>future rebellion</u> in the north by <u>destroying</u> the rebels' <u>supplies</u> and sources of <u>support</u>. The Harrying also sent a powerful <u>message</u> to the rest of the country about what to expect if they <u>rebelled</u>.

William Punished the Anglo-Saxons Harshly

People at the time <u>criticised</u> William for the Harrying of the North. The 12th-century historian <u>Orderic Vitalis</u> wrote 'I have often praised William... but I can say <u>nothing good</u> about this <u>brutal slaughter</u>. God will <u>punish</u> him.'

1) During the winter of <u>1069-1070</u>, William and his army marched across the north of England, <u>burning villages</u> and <u>slaughtering</u> their inhabitants.

2) They also caused a <u>famine</u> by deliberately <u>destroying food supplies</u> and <u>livestock</u> — these <u>tactics</u> are often referred to as '<u>scorched earth</u>' tactics.

3) According to one <u>12th-century source</u>, there was <u>so little food</u> available after the Harrying of the North that the remaining Anglo-Saxons had to eat <u>dogs</u>, <u>cats</u> and <u>horses</u> to <u>survive</u>.

4) This <u>destruction</u> stretched across a huge area. While the <u>majority</u> of the Harrying took place in <u>Yorkshire</u> and the <u>north east</u>, the damage also reached <u>Lincolnshire</u>, <u>Cheshire</u> and <u>Staffordshire</u>.

- The Harrying is often seen as evidence of the '<u>Norman Yoke</u>'. This refers to the idea that the Normans <u>brutally oppressed</u> the Anglo-Saxons using methods that were <u>unnecessarily cruel</u>.
- However, <u>laying waste</u> to <u>enemy territory</u> was a <u>common military tactic</u> in the 11th century. Some historians argue that we shouldn't <u>judge</u> William's actions by <u>modern moral standards</u>.

The Harrying had Short-Term and Long-Term Consequences

1) It's clear from the sources that the <u>Harrying of the North</u> was a <u>brutal</u> campaign which caused <u>suffering</u> for those who were caught up in it.

2) In the <u>short term</u>, many northerners <u>fled</u> from the destruction and became <u>refugees</u>, settling elsewhere in England or the south of Scotland. The people who <u>stayed</u> in the north faced <u>disease</u> and <u>starvation</u>.

3) Some northerners joined other <u>pockets of resistance</u> such as Hereward the Wake's East Anglian rebellion (see p.22), but the resistance didn't last for long.

4) In 1086, many northern villages were described as '<u>waste</u>' in the <u>Domesday Book</u> (see p.36). Some historians use this to argue that the Harrying led to <u>long-term damage</u> to the <u>northern economy</u>, as the Domesday Book was made almost <u>twenty years later</u>.

Comment and Analysis

There were other reasons why a village may have been described as '<u>waste</u>' in the <u>Domesday Book</u> (e.g. if it didn't pay <u>taxes</u>), so it's difficult to assess whether or not the <u>Harrying</u> caused any serious <u>long-term damage</u>.

The Harrying of the North

Use the activities on this page to really nail down what you've learnt about the Harrying of the North.

Knowledge and Understanding

1) In your own words, explain what the Harrying of the North was.

2) Using the key words below, explain why William carried out the Harrying of the North.

deter   threat   rebellions   supplies

Interpretation

This interpretation shows Norman soldiers attacking an Anglo-Saxon village.

a) Anglo-Saxon buildings on fire.

b) A Norman soldier chasing cows.

Use pages 18 and 20 to help you answer question 2.

1) Do you think each of the labelled features above is convincing about how William treated the Anglo-Saxons after the 1069 revolt? Explain your answer for each feature.

2) Does this interpretation give a complete view of how William treated Anglo-Saxons who rebelled against him? Explain your answer.

Thinking Historically

1) Copy and complete the mind map below, listing the consequences of the Harrying of the North.

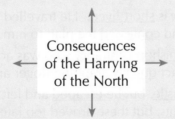

Consequences of the Harrying of the North

2) Do you think William could have maintained control of England without the Harrying of the North? Explain your answer. You can use other pages in this section to help you.

The Anglo-Saxons had got on William's last nerve...

Planning answers to exam questions can be a good way to revise — if you can't think of much to write when you're planning an answer, it might mean that you need to recap the topic.

Resistance to Norman Rule, 1070-1075

The last of the resistance to William came from <u>Hereward the Wake</u>, followed by some of William's <u>own earls</u>.

Hereward the Wake led an East Anglian Rebellion

1) In <u>1070</u>, there was an uprising in <u>East Anglia</u> led by an <u>Anglo-Saxon thegn</u> (see p.28) known as <u>Hereward the Wake</u>. Hereward's lands had been <u>confiscated</u> after the Norman Conquest.

2) Hereward was <u>supported</u> by the Danes, who had arrived in East Anglia in 1070. However, William paid the Danes to make them <u>abandon Hereward</u>.

3) In <u>1071</u>, Hereward was joined by more Anglo-Saxon rebels, including <u>Morcar</u> (see p.18). They went to the <u>Isle of Ely</u> and tried to hold it against William's army.

4) William's forces <u>besieged</u> the island and <u>defeated</u> the rebels. Morcar was <u>captured</u> and <u>imprisoned</u>.

5) Hereward <u>survived</u> the attack on Ely, but <u>not much</u> is known about his fate afterwards. However, he doesn't seem to have taken part in <u>any further resistance</u>. Hereward's uprising was the <u>last major rebellion</u> to happen until 1075 (see below).

Some sources on Hereward the Wake say that he <u>surrendered</u> to William, who <u>pardoned</u> him.

© Mary Evans Picture Library/

Some of William's Earls started to Resent Him

1) In 1071, <u>William FitzOsbern</u> (one of the king's <u>closest allies</u>) <u>died</u>. FitzOsbern was the <u>Earl of Hereford</u>, but he also held other lands in the <u>south</u> and <u>west</u> of the country. This made him a <u>very powerful</u> figure.

2) FitzOsbern's lands and titles were all <u>inherited</u> by his son, <u>Roger de Breteuil</u>. However, Roger was <u>unhappy</u> because he believed he didn't have the same <u>power</u> and <u>influence</u> as his father.

3) The <u>Earl of East Anglia</u>, <u>Ralph de Gael</u>, was similarly unhappy with the king. He had also inherited his father's earldom, but felt that his <u>power</u> and <u>influence</u> were being <u>limited</u>. ———→

> The Revolt of the Earls was <u>different</u> from the <u>other rebellions</u> because the rebels weren't all <u>Anglo-Saxons</u>. Roger de Breteuil was a <u>Norman</u>, and Ralph de Gael was originally from <u>Brittany</u> (a region in northern France).

4) In 1075, Ralph <u>married</u> Roger's sister, Emma. At the <u>wedding</u>, the two earls joined forces with <u>Earl Waltheof of Northumbria</u> (an <u>Anglo-Saxon</u>) and started to plan a revolt against the king.

The Revolt of the Earls went Wrong from the Start

1) Waltheof's involvement in the revolt was <u>short-lived</u>. He travelled to <u>Normandy</u> to meet <u>King William</u> and <u>confessed</u> the plan to him.

2) William gave the information to <u>Archbishop Lanfranc</u>, who was acting as <u>regent</u> (see p.24) in <u>England</u>. This allowed Lanfranc to react <u>quickly</u>, trapping Roger and Ralph in their earldoms.

3) Ralph was under siege in <u>Norwich Castle</u>, but he <u>escaped</u> and left his wife (Emma) in control. He went to <u>Denmark</u> for <u>reinforcements</u>, but these arrived <u>too late</u>. After a long siege, Emma <u>surrendered</u>. She and Ralph agreed to <u>give up</u> their <u>lands</u> in East Anglia, then went into <u>exile</u>.

4) Meanwhile, Roger barely made it out of Hereford. He was <u>captured</u> by William's supporters, then <u>imprisoned</u> for life for his <u>disloyalty</u> to the king.

Comment and Analysis

It's <u>uncertain</u> why Waltheof was punished <u>more harshly</u> than Roger and Ralph. Anglo-Saxons (e.g. Edwin and Morcar, see p.18) had rebelled against the king in the past, but William treated them <u>more leniently</u>.

5) Despite <u>confessing</u>, <u>Waltheof</u> was <u>beheaded</u> for taking part in the revolt. He became the <u>only</u> member of the Anglo-Saxon nobility to be <u>executed</u> in William's reign.

6) The Revolt of the Earls was the <u>last major rebellion</u> to involve <u>Anglo-Saxons</u> in William's reign. After Waltheof's <u>execution</u>, they may have realised they had <u>no choice</u> but to <u>cooperate</u> with the <u>Normans</u>.

Resistance to Norman Rule, 1070-1075

SKILLS PRACTICE

Test your knowledge of the rebellions William faced during his reign as king with these activities.

Knowledge and Understanding

1) Copy and complete the flowchart below, adding the missing information about the rebellion led by Hereward the Wake in 1070-1071.

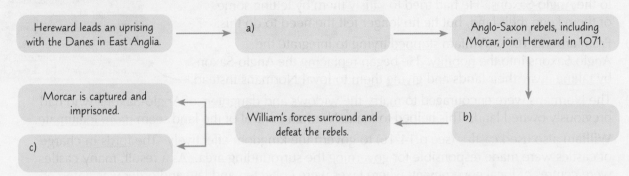

| Hereward leads an uprising with the Danes in East Anglia. | → | a) | → | Anglo-Saxon rebels, including Morcar, join Hereward in 1071. |

| Morcar is captured and imprisoned. | ← | William's forces surround and defeat the rebels. | ← | b) |

c)

2) Why did Roger de Breteuil and Ralph de Gael decide to revolt in 1075?

3) Make a flashcard for each person or group of people below. Write their name on one side and describe their role in the Revolt of the Earls on the other.

   a) Roger de Breteuil   c) Emma de Gael   e) Archbishop Lanfranc

   b) Ralph de Gael   d) Earl Waltheof   f) The Danes

4) Explain how Waltheof's punishment was different from Roger de Breteuil's and Ralph de Gael's.

Thinking Historically

1) Why do you think the Revolt of the Earls was the last major rebellion against William to involve the Anglo-Saxons?

2) Explain why each of the factors below made the Revolt of the Earls a threat to William's rule.

   a) The rebels weren't all Anglo-Saxons.   b) The earls held a lot of land between them.   c) William was in Normandy at the time of the revolt.

EXAM TIP

William was disgusted by the revolting Earls...

Make sure you don't mix up the details of the different rebellions. For example, Hereward the Wake rebelled in East Anglia in 1070, whereas the Revolt of the Earls took place in 1075.

William I and William II

William I brought a little stability to England by defeating rebellions, but he needed to find a way to maintain it. He did such a good job that William II didn't need to change much at all.

William I maintained control in Different Ways

1) The rebellions at the start of William I's reign changed his attitude to the Anglo-Saxons. He had tried to satisfy them by letting some of them keep their land, but he no longer felt the need to do this.

2) From around 1070, William stopped trying to integrate the Anglo-Saxons into the nobility. He began replacing the Anglo-Saxons by taking away their lands and giving them to loyal Normans instead.

> The redistribution of land is one example of a process known as Normanisation. William made England 'more Norman' by replacing Anglo-Saxons with Normans in areas such as government and the Church.

3) The Normans were encouraged to marry the widows and daughters of Anglo-Saxons who had previously owned land. This helped to make Norman control of the land seem more legitimate.

4) William also used castles (see p.14-16) to govern the kingdom effectively. The lords in charge of castles were made responsible for governing the surrounding area. As a result, many castles were centres of local government, where taxes were collected and law and order was enforced.

5) Having established his authority in England, William felt comfortable going back to Normandy. He used regents to govern England during these absences, such as Archbishop Lanfranc of Canterbury (see p.48).

> A regent is someone who rules on the king's behalf, with the same authority as the king.

William II was the next King of England

1) On 9th September 1087, William I died from a serious injury while at war with the King of France. His sons inherited his lands and wealth:

- His eldest son, Robert Curthose, became Duke of Normandy.
- His second son, William Rufus, became King of England.
- His third son, Henry, received £5000 (a huge sum of money).

> It was Norman custom for the eldest son to inherit everything (see p.30). However, Robert had rebelled against William in the past and they had a hostile relationship. This might have led William to break with tradition by sharing his inheritance between his sons.

2) William Rufus had been with his father in France, but sailed for England a couple of days before he died. He quickly gained the support of Archbishop Lanfranc, who crowned him William II on 26th September.

3) Robert went to Normandy and was accepted as duke. However, he believed that William had wrongfully seized the throne of England.

4) Robert wasn't the only one who thought that William shouldn't be King of England. Many Norman lords also thought that, as the eldest son, Robert should have inherited England as well as Normandy. These lords included Odo of Bayeux, who was Robert and William's uncle. In 1088, Odo started a rebellion to replace William with Robert.

Comment and Analysis

Many lords held land in England and Normandy, so they had to serve both William and Robert — they thought their lives would be easier if England and Normandy were united under one ruler rather than dividing their loyalties between two competing rulers.

5) However, Odo's rebellion failed. Most of the lords in England were loyal to William, and Robert didn't send Odo reinforcements from Normandy. As punishment for his betrayal, William sent Odo into exile.

William II inherited a Well-Governed Kingdom

1) William II didn't have a lot of experience in government, and he lacked the innovation of his father. He inherited a system that was working well, so he didn't change it much.

2) William exploited the existing system of government for personal gain. He earned a lot of money through heavy taxation and took even more wealth from the Church (see p.52).

3) He continued to fight against Robert until 1096, when Robert gave Normandy to William. This meant that William was in control of both Normandy and England.

William I and William II

After all William I's hard work to stabilise England, he was succeeded by his son, William Rufus, who became King William II. Have a go at these activities to make sure you know William I from William II.

Knowledge and Understanding

1) How did William I's attitude towards the Anglo-Saxons change as a result of the rebellions between 1068 and 1071?

2) Explain what is meant by the term 'Normanisation'.

3) What did each of William I's sons inherit from him?

4) Copy and complete the timeline below about William II's reign as King of England. Fill in all of the key events between 1087 and 1096, giving as much detail as possible.

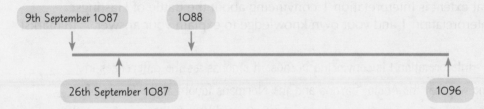

5) Why did Odo's rebellion fail? Explain your answer.

Thinking Historically

1) Copy and complete the table below, explaining how each of the following helped William I to maintain control of England.

	How this helped William I to maintain control
a) Normanisation	
b) Marriages	
c) Castles	
d) Regents	

William II — the cash grab sequel to William I...

Make sure the points you make in an answer are relevant to the question — you could write about William II for a question about the succession in 1087, but not for one about Hastings.

The Normans: Conquest and Control

Worked Exam-Style Question

This page will give you a good idea of how to tackle the interpretation question in the exam.

Interpretation 1

The Anglo-Saxon army and the Norman army face each other at the Battle of Hastings.

To what extent is Interpretation 1 convincing about the Battle of Hastings?
Use Interpretation 1 and your own knowledge to explain your answer.   [8 marks]

The <u>first</u> <u>sentence</u> in <u>each paragraph</u> briefly states whether the interpretation is convincing and why.

Using <u>technical</u> <u>terms</u> shows a strong understanding of the topic.

This uses <u>knowledge</u> of the <u>Battle of Hastings</u> to show what is <u>missing</u> from the interpretation.

Interpretation 1 is convincing because it emphasises the differences in the way that the Anglo-Saxons and the Normans fought at the Battle of Hastings. The image depicts the Anglo-Saxon soldiers fighting on foot and the Normans charging towards them on horseback. This is convincing because the Anglo-Saxon army was almost entirely made up of foot-soldiers, whereas the cavalry was an important part of the Norman army. The Norman cavalry are portrayed as fierce and powerful, reflecting their ability to attack with greater speed and strength than the Anglo-Saxon foot-soldiers. However, the interpretation is only partially convincing because it does not give a complete picture of either side's army. The interpretation does not distinguish between the housecarls and the fyrd in the Anglo-Saxon army, and it does not show that the Normans used foot-soldiers as well as cavalry.

The interpretation is convincing because it shows the Normans breaking through the Anglo-Saxon shield wall. The image depicts Anglo-Saxon soldiers forming a shield wall by standing in rows with their shields locked together. This tactic was often used by the Anglo-Saxons in battle, including at the Battle of Hastings. The image also shows Anglo-Saxon soldiers on their hands and knees about to be overrun by the Norman cavalry, reflecting the fact that the Normans managed to break the shield wall during the Battle of Hastings. However, the interpretation does not show that the Normans broke through the shield wall by using the feigned flight tactic, pretending to run away to draw out Anglo-Saxon soldiers from the shield wall formation. Therefore the interpretation is only partially convincing about how the Normans defeated the Anglo-Saxons at the Battle of Hastings.

This refers to the <u>details</u> of the image to work out what it is trying to <u>show</u> or <u>say</u>.

This judges how <u>accurately</u> the image represents the Battle of Hastings.

The Normans: Conquest and Control

Exam-Style Questions

This page will help you to practise the 8-mark questions that you'll be asked in the exam.

Interpretation 1

> The Conqueror's second son, William Rufus, moved quickly to claim the English throne as his own. Did he anticipate the discontent that would result from his actions, or did he imagine he would be welcomed with open arms as the rightful King of England? Whatever his thoughts, William Rufus's controversial claim to the throne became a great source of tension both among his nobles and within his own family.

Exam-Style Questions

1) To what extent is Interpretation 1 convincing about the challenges William II faced when he became King of England? Use Interpretation 1 and your own knowledge to explain your answer. [8 marks]

2) How were castles important for Norman England? Explain your answer. [8 marks]

3) Give an account of how William I's response to rebellions changed. [8 marks]

Norman Society

William I established his rule through a mixture of <u>change</u> and <u>continuity</u> from the <u>Anglo-Saxon</u> system.

Anglo-Saxon Society had a Clear Hierarchy

1) Since the 9th century, Anglo-Saxon England had been a <u>single kingdom</u> that was ruled by <u>one king</u>. The <u>king</u> was the <u>richest</u> person in the kingdom and he owned the <u>largest</u> amount of <u>land</u>. He was responsible for <u>protecting</u> the country from <u>invaders</u> and overseeing the <u>running</u> of the country as <u>head</u> of the <u>government</u>.

2) The <u>most powerful</u> men in the <u>nobility</u> were the <u>earls</u>, who were given <u>large areas of land</u> (<u>earldoms</u>) by the <u>king</u>. In return, earls were expected to make sure their earldoms were <u>well governed</u>.

3) The <u>less powerful</u> members of the nobility were called <u>thegns</u>. They received <u>smaller areas of land</u> from their <u>lord</u> (who would be either the king or an earl). In return, thegns helped to <u>govern</u> the <u>local area</u> and provided <u>military service</u>.

4) Most of the population were <u>peasants</u> who did <u>agricultural work</u> for their <u>lord</u> and were given a <u>small plot of land</u> in return. Some peasants were <u>slaves</u> — workers who could be <u>bought and sold</u> and didn't have any <u>land</u> of their <u>own</u>.

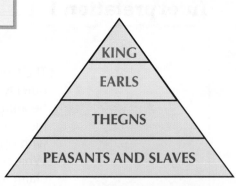

Even though the king was the <u>most powerful</u> person in society, he couldn't rule without the <u>support</u> of the <u>upper nobility</u> (earls) and the <u>lower nobility</u> (thegns).

The word '<u>lord</u>' refers to anyone who had other people <u>relying</u> on them for <u>land</u> and <u>protection</u> (dependents). <u>Not all</u> lords were <u>wealthy</u> or <u>high up</u> in the hierarchy. Dependents often had to <u>fight</u> or <u>work</u> for their lords.

Comment and Analysis

The peasant class (or <u>peasantry</u>) was a <u>diverse group</u>. Some peasants were wealthier than others, and not all of them lived the <u>same lifestyle</u>.

William I Changed the Social Structure of England

1) After 1066, William kept the Anglo-Saxon idea of <u>giving out land</u> in exchange for <u>service</u>. However, he <u>changed</u> the <u>structure</u> of the <u>existing system</u> so the <u>king</u> had full <u>control</u> and <u>ownership</u> of all land in the kingdom, which he could <u>give out</u> or <u>take away</u> as he wished.

2) These changes were intended to create a <u>network</u> of <u>loyal supporters</u> who could provide <u>military service</u> to the king, which was crucial in helping William to <u>secure the conquest</u>.

3) Historians often refer to the new social structure as the <u>feudal system</u>. There was a <u>clear hierarchy</u>, like in Anglo-Saxon England, but some of the roles <u>changed slightly</u>.

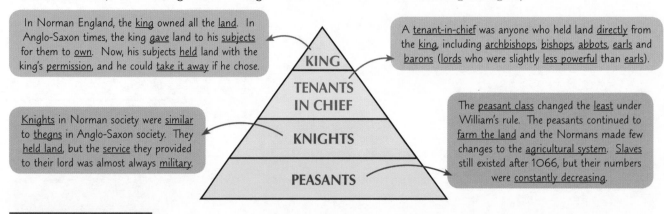

In Norman England, the <u>king</u> owned all the <u>land</u>. In Anglo-Saxon times, the king <u>gave</u> land to his <u>subjects</u> for them to <u>own</u>. Now, his subjects <u>held</u> land with the king's <u>permission</u>, and he could <u>take it away</u> if he chose.

A <u>tenant-in-chief</u> was anyone who held land <u>directly</u> from the <u>king</u>, including <u>archbishops</u>, <u>bishops</u>, <u>abbots</u>, <u>earls</u> and <u>barons</u> (lords who were slightly <u>less powerful</u> than <u>earls</u>).

Knights in Norman society were <u>similar</u> to <u>thegns</u> in Anglo-Saxon society. They <u>held land</u>, but the <u>service</u> they provided to their lord was almost always <u>military</u>.

The <u>peasant class</u> changed the <u>least</u> under William's rule. The peasants continued to <u>farm the land</u> and the Normans made few changes to the <u>agricultural system</u>. <u>Slaves</u> still existed after 1066, but their numbers were <u>constantly decreasing</u>.

Comment and Analysis

The idea of giving land to someone and becoming their lord is an example of <u>patronage</u>. However, patronage didn't always involve land — it's a general term for the <u>support</u> that someone provided to a <u>person</u> or an <u>organisation</u>. Other examples of patronage include the <u>power</u> and <u>influence</u> that William I gave to his <u>followers</u>, or the <u>money</u> and <u>protection</u> that nobles gave to the <u>Church</u>.

Norman Society

There's a lot of information on the previous page about Anglo-Saxon society and Norman society. Have a go at these activities to practise what you've learnt and to make sure everything has really sunk in.

Knowledge and Understanding

1) Using the key words below, describe the role of the king in Anglo-Saxon England.

   invaders   government   land   nobility

2) Copy and complete the table below. State whether each type of person was part of the social hierarchy in Anglo-Saxon England, Norman England or both, then give as much information as you can about each type of person.

	Anglo-Saxon, Norman or both	Information
a) Tenants-in-chief		
b) Earls		
c) Thegns		
d) Knights		

3) Explain what the following terms mean:

   a) Lord   b) Patronage   c) Feudal system

Thinking Historically

1) Copy and complete the table below, explaining whether there was change or continuity in each aspect of society between Anglo-Saxon England and Norman England.

Aspect of society	Change or continuity?	Explanation for choice
a) Ownership of land		
b) Work done by peasants		
c) Number of slaves		

2) Why was the feudal system important for William's control over England? Explain your answer.

I didn't realise the Anglo-Saxons made pyramids as well...

It's good to know how things changed or stayed the same, but you should also learn why this was the case — e.g. William changed how society was structured to give himself more control.

Life Under the Normans

Lordship and Landholding

Under William I, only those who were <u>loyal</u> to the <u>king</u> and their <u>lord</u> were allowed to hold on to their <u>land</u>.

The Feudal System was designed to Reward Loyal Service

1) The <u>feudal system</u> (see p.28) was based on <u>vassalic bonds</u>. The <u>king</u> and his <u>lords</u> gave <u>land</u> to their subjects (<u>vassals</u>) in return for <u>loyalty</u>.

2) Tenants-in-chief were the <u>king's vassals</u>. They did <u>homage</u> to the king by <u>kneeling</u> before him and <u>swearing loyalty</u> to him. They also provided <u>knights</u> when the king needed them and <u>shared</u> a portion of the <u>income</u> from their land with him.

3) Knights were the <u>tenants-in-chief's vassals</u>. In return for <u>land</u>, knights had to do <u>homage</u> and pay <u>taxes</u>, as well as providing <u>military service</u> to their lord. This service might involve <u>protecting a castle</u>, <u>fighting in wars</u> or <u>keeping their lord safe</u> while travelling.

4) Most <u>peasants</u> worked for a lord by giving <u>labour service</u> on his land. In return, they were given their lord's <u>protection</u> and the right to <u>farm</u> a <u>small patch of land</u> for themselves. However, they had to pay <u>taxes</u> and give their lord a <u>share</u> of their <u>crops</u>. Peasants didn't formally do <u>homage</u> to their lord, but they were still expected to stay <u>loyal</u> to him.

> If a vassal <u>broke the agreement</u> between them and their lord, they might be forced to <u>forfeit</u> (give up) their <u>land</u>.

© 19th era / Alamy Stock Photo

The Anglo-Saxon Elite was Replaced with Normans

1) After 1066, William I tried to work with the Anglo-Saxon <u>nobility</u> by allowing them to <u>keep</u> their <u>land</u> if they <u>accepted</u> his rule. However, he <u>gave up</u> on this approach after a series of <u>rebellions</u> (see p.18-22).

2) Around <u>1070</u>, William started to <u>systematically replace</u> Anglo-Saxon nobles with Normans. The Domesday Book (see p.36) shows almost <u>all</u> the Anglo-Saxon elite had been <u>replaced</u> with Normans by <u>1086</u>.

3) William <u>rewarded</u> his most important supporters with <u>land</u>, making them <u>tenants-in-chief</u> (see p.28). The tenants-in-chief kept some of this land for <u>themselves</u> then passed the rest of it on to their <u>vassals</u>.

4) William also <u>changed</u> the <u>size</u> and <u>shape</u> of estates. In Anglo-Saxon England, some lords had held <u>vast areas of land</u>, whereas others had held lands that were <u>scattered</u> across <u>several shires</u>. William <u>reorganised</u> these large areas of land into much <u>smaller estates</u> that were limited to <u>a single region</u>.

5) These changes helped William to <u>maintain control</u> because <u>smaller estates</u> were much easier to <u>defend</u>. Giving noble families smaller areas of land also <u>strengthened</u> William's own position. By <u>restricting</u> the <u>power</u> of these families, he made sure <u>none</u> of them were <u>strong</u> enough to <u>threaten</u> his position as king.

Comment and Analysis

William had a small '<u>inner circle</u>' of <u>loyal supporters</u> who held around a <u>quarter</u> of England, but even these lands weren't as big as the <u>earldoms</u> (e.g. Northumbria and Mercia) that had existed in <u>Anglo-Saxon England</u>.

The Normans introduced Primogeniture to England

1) In Anglo-Saxon England, it was common to <u>divide land equally</u> between each of a landholder's <u>children</u> when he died. However, the Normans used a system of <u>inheritance</u> called <u>primogeniture</u>, meaning land was inherited by a landholder's <u>eldest son</u> — if a landholder died <u>childless</u>, the land returned to his lord.

2) Primogeniture helped to <u>limit landholding</u> to <u>fewer people</u>. It also prevented a family's estates from becoming <u>small</u> and <u>fragmented</u>.

3) Primogeniture was also a way for the king and other lords to <u>make money</u> — a landholder's eldest son had to <u>pay</u> a tax to the lord to <u>inherit</u> the land, otherwise it was <u>seized</u>. This was known as <u>relief</u>.

> This tax is one of several ways that lords were able to gain <u>extra income</u> from their land — these are known as <u>feudal incidents</u>.

Lordship and Landholding

These activities will help you understand the effect of William's changes to landholding in England.

Interpretation

The interpretation below is about the feudal system in Norman England.

> The Norman Conquest shook things up in English society because it introduced the feudal system. Loyalty and land were at the centre of this system, and everyone from earls to peasants had a role to play. In return for land, men were expected to provide their lords with financial and military support. Even those who didn't officially bend the knee still owed their lord service and loyalty if they wanted to survive.

1) Explain whether the interpretation is convincing about the following subjects. You can use the information from pages 28 and 30 to help you.

   a) The role of vassals in the feudal system

   b) The role of peasants in the feudal system

   c) The importance of loyalty in the feudal system

Knowledge and Understanding

1) Explain how the lands held by William's 'inner circle' of loyal supporters compared to the lands held by earls in Anglo-Saxon England.

2) Explain how the Norman system of inheritance was different from the Anglo-Saxon system of inheritance.

Thinking Historically

1) Why do you think the Anglo-Saxon rebellions (see pages 18-22) encouraged William to replace Anglo-Saxon nobles with Norman nobles?

2) Explain how William's redistribution of land helped him to maintain control over England. You can use the factors in the boxes below to help you write your answer.

   size of estates   power of noble families

3) Copy and complete the mind map below by explaining how primogeniture affected each aspect of Norman England.

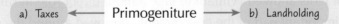

   a) Taxes ←——— Primogeniture ———→ b) Landholding

The royalty demanded loyalty...

When you're writing in the exam, only use the most relevant examples to back up your points. There should be a clear link between the examples you use and the point you're making.

Norman Government

William I was happy with the existing system of government in England, so he kept quite a lot of it the same.

The Nobility and Sheriffs helped to Govern England

The king used major landholders and royal officials to help him govern the kingdom:

- The tenants-in-chief (see p.28) oversaw the government in their own lands. These covered relatively large areas, making tenants-in-chief very powerful.
- The tenants-in-chief's lands were divided into shires (a bit like modern counties). These shires were governed by royal officials called sheriffs.
- The shires were divided up into smaller areas called hundreds. These were made up of multiple villages, and were also controlled by the sheriffs and their deputies.

> The idea of dividing the country into shires and hundreds was carried over from the Anglo-Saxon system of government.

Sheriffs had an Increased Role in Local Government

1) The role of sheriff had existed in Anglo-Saxon England, and it didn't change a lot under the Normans — they helped to govern at a local level. Their role included:

- Supervising the collection of fines and taxes
- Judging civil or criminal cases in local courts (see p.34)
- Organising (and often leading) military forces

> **Comment and Analysis**
>
> Giving more power to sheriffs meant that earls had less influence over how their lands were managed. This led to resentment — some historians believe it was one of the main reasons for the Revolt of the Earls in 1075 (see p.22).

2) In Anglo-Saxon England, the earls (see p.28) had also performed some of these duties. However, there were fewer earls under the Normans, and William I had reduced their authority. This meant that the sheriffs were able to perform their duties with less interference from the earls.

3) When William took control of all the land in England (see p.28), he kept around one quarter of it for his personal use — this land was called the royal demesne. One new responsibility for sheriffs was to manage the royal demesne, which hadn't existed in Anglo-Saxon England.

4) As in Anglo-Saxon England, sheriffs were directly appointed by the king. However, William usually appointed people who were wealthier and held more land than Anglo-Saxon sheriffs.

5) William had to be careful about giving the sheriffs too much power. They needed enough authority to perform their duties, but they might be able to rebel against the king if they became too powerful.

William I's Government became More Centralised

1) England was already a centralised kingdom when the Normans invaded. William kept the structure of the existing government, but filled it with Normans rather than Anglo-Saxons. William also used certain features of Anglo-Saxon government more effectively.

> Centralisation is when power becomes focused around a single figure — in this case, the king.

2) For example, William increased the use of writs (short documents containing royal commands for local government officials to follow). These were common in Anglo-Saxon England, but hadn't been used in Normandy. The use of writs allowed William to take a more direct role in running the whole kingdom.

3) The chancery was an important part of the government. It moved around the country with the king, and was responsible for producing documents (including writs) that were needed to help the king to govern. There wasn't a chancery in Normandy before 1066, so the idea may have come from the Anglo-Saxons.

4) The Curia Regis was the king's council. It was made up of the king's tenants-in-chief, who advised him and helped him to govern the kingdom. This was similar to the Witan in Anglo-Saxon England (see p.8).

5) The treasury was responsible for managing royal income. It also physically stored the king's own wealth.

Norman Government

William's changes were great for sheriffs, but not everyone did so well out of these developments. Give these activities a go to make sure you know who benefited from the changes to Norman government.

Knowledge and Understanding

1) Using the key words below, explain how the king used the nobility and royal officials to govern England.

tenants-in-chief   sheriffs   deputies   shires   hundreds

2) How did changes to the roles of sheriffs and earls affect William's relationship with his earls?

3) In your own words, explain what the royal demesne was.

4) Why did William need to limit how much power he gave to sheriffs?

5) Explain what is meant by a centralised government.

6) Explain the following features of William's government. Give as much detail as possible.

a) Curia Regis   b) Chancery   c) Treasury

Thinking Historically

1) Copy and complete the table below, giving ways that sheriffs changed and ways that they stayed the same from Anglo-Saxon England to Norman England.

Change	Continuity

2) How did the following aspects of the government change from Anglo-Saxon England to Norman England? Explain how each change increased William's control.

a) Writs   b) People

William took control through centralisation...

William was arguably a successful ruler, but not all of his decisions helped him maintain control — it's important to know how the changes he made as King of England impacted his reign.

The Norman Legal System

The Normans didn't change much about the legal system, but they introduced a few new ideas of their own.

The Normans Didn't make Major Changes to English Law

1) When he became king, William I promised that he wouldn't change the laws that had existed during King Edward's reign. The Anglo-Saxon legal system was well developed, and there was no need to change a system that worked well.

2) As a result, the laws of England were very similar before and after 1066. However, William did introduce some new laws:

> **Comment and Analysis**
>
> Maintaining pre-conquest law was a good way for William I to create continuity with King Edward's reign and show that he was Edward's legitimate successor.

- He introduced forest law, which set aside large areas of the country as 'royal forest' for the king to hunt in.

- The royal forest wasn't just woodland — it included any land that was set aside as hunting grounds. Ordinary people weren't allowed to use the royal forest, and they faced severe punishment for breaking the law.

- William also introduced the 'murdrum' fine to protect Norman settlers from violence. If a Norman was murdered and the killer wasn't caught, then the whole village where he was murdered had to pay a large fine.

> The 'murdrum' fine was introduced to protect Norman settlers in the first years of the conquest. However, the law remained throughout William's reign as it was a useful source of income for the king.

3) One problem with the Anglo-Saxon legal system was that courts in different parts of the country often operated in different ways. The Normans made their legal system more consistent across the country.

Accused Criminals were tried in Courts...

1) The king's court was the highest court in the land, where the most important legal cases were heard. Some of these cases were dealt with by the king himself, but others were dealt with by royal officials.

> In Anglo-Saxon England, the shire courts and hundred courts were the main way of delivering royal justice at a local level, and this continued under the Normans. These types of court hadn't existed in Normandy, but the Normans must have found them useful and decided to keep them in place.

2) The shire courts tried criminal cases and dealt with cases involving land and property. They were usually overseen by sheriffs and attended by important people in the shire such as major landholders and senior churchmen.

3) For less serious crimes, like stealing livestock or failing to repay small debts, there were also courts called hundred courts. These were overseen by sheriffs or their deputies.

4) The shire courts and hundred courts were public courts that delivered royal justice, but the Normans also used other courts where lords dealt with disputes in their own lands. There were manor courts to deal with everyday problems in villages (see p.38), like peasants who weren't working properly, and the Normans introduced new honourial courts to resolve land disputes between a lord's vassals.

... but the Normans also used Trials by Ordeal or Combat

1) If a court couldn't come to a verdict, a trial by ordeal was often used to decide whether someone was innocent or guilty. This wasn't a new idea — it was a custom in England and Normandy before 1066.

2) There were different types of ordeal. For example, someone accused of a crime might be thrown into water that had been blessed by a priest. If they floated, the water (and therefore God) was 'rejecting' them, meaning they were guilty. If they sank, the water was 'accepting' them, so they were innocent.

3) The Normans introduced trial by combat to England. If someone was accused of a crime, they were allowed to challenge the accuser to a fight to the death. The Normans thought that if someone was innocent, then God would intervene and help them to win the fight.

The Norman Legal System

The Normans affected the legal system in England in a number of ways, but they also kept some things the same. To help you think about how the legal system was affected, have a go at the activities on this page.

Knowledge and Understanding

1) Explain what is meant by each of the following terms:

    a) Forest law   b) Murdrum fine

2) Copy and complete the table below, giving the types of cases and crimes that were taken to each court and who was in charge of each court. Give as much detail as possible.

Court	Cases and crimes	Who was in charge
a) King's Court		
b) Shire Court		
c) Hundred Court		
d) Manor Court		
e) Honourial Court		

3) Explain how each of these trials was carried out and how guilt was determined.

    a) Trial by ordeal   b) Trial by combat

Thinking Historically

1) How did each of the following aspects of the English legal system change from Anglo-Saxon England to Norman England? How did they stay the same?

    a) English law   b) Courts   c) Trials

2) Copy and complete the mind map below, giving different reasons why the Normans kept many aspects of the Anglo-Saxon legal system the same after the conquest. Give as much detail as possible.

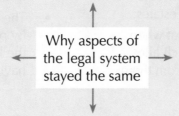

Why aspects of the legal system stayed the same

The Normans fined Anglo-Saxons for trying to murdrum...

While it's important to recognise the changes that the Normans made to aspects of English life, you also need to know what they kept the same from Anglo-Saxon England and why.

The Domesday Book

The Domesday Book is a detailed <u>survey</u> and <u>valuation</u> of England's <u>land</u> and <u>resources</u>. No other public record on a similar scale was created in England until the <u>1800s</u>, so William I was really ahead of his time...

The Domesday Book records Who owned What

1) In <u>December 1085</u>, William ordered a <u>survey</u> of all the <u>land</u> in England, which was carried out in <u>1086</u>. This was known as the <u>Domesday Survey</u>.

2) The survey recorded the amount of <u>land</u> held by the <u>king</u>, his <u>tenants-in-chief</u> and their <u>vassals</u> (see p.30). It also noted who held the land in <u>1066</u> (before the Norman Conquest), how much it was worth then, and its <u>value</u> in <u>1086</u>.

Comment and Analysis
The <u>Domesday Survey</u> was only possible thanks to Anglo-Saxon <u>taxation records</u> and <u>systems</u> of <u>government</u>, such as the way the kingdom was <u>divided</u> into <u>shires</u> and <u>hundreds</u> (see p.32).

3) The survey was written down in the <u>Domesday Book</u> — as it contains information from both <u>before</u> and <u>after</u> 1066, the Domesday Book is an important source for studying the <u>impact of the conquest</u>.

The Domesday Book took a lot of Organisation

1) To carry out the <u>survey</u>, the <u>tenants-in-chief</u> and <u>government officials</u> in each <u>shire</u> made <u>lists</u> of who owned the land, and <u>commissioners</u> were appointed to compare these lists with <u>existing records</u>.

2) <u>Juries</u> taken from each <u>hundred</u> were called to special meetings of the <u>shire courts</u>, where the commissioners asked them about the <u>ownership</u> and <u>value</u> of the land.

© Mary Evans / The National

3) These juries were made up of <u>equal numbers</u> of <u>Anglo-Saxons</u> and <u>Normans</u>. This allowed the commissioners to gather <u>accurate information</u> from both <u>before</u> and <u>after</u> the conquest.

4) All the information was then recorded in the <u>Great Domesday Book</u> (usually called the <u>Domesday Book</u>).

The information helped to Govern the Kingdom

The <u>Domesday Book</u> provided the king with <u>financial</u>, <u>legal</u> and <u>military</u> information:

Financial

- The Domesday Book allowed the king to make sure that he was receiving all the <u>taxes</u> and other <u>payments</u> that his subjects owed him.
- By creating a detailed record of <u>who owned what</u> and <u>how much their lands were worth</u>, the king could decide whether or not to demand <u>more taxes</u> from certain estates.
- It also helped the king to figure out when someone had <u>inherited</u> land, which allowed him to demand <u>relief</u> (see p.30) from them.

Legal

- Between 1066 and 1086, there had been <u>constant disagreement</u> between Normans and Anglo-Saxons about <u>landownership</u>.
- By creating a detailed record of <u>who owned what</u>, the king could <u>end the disagreements</u> and <u>legalise</u> Norman ownership of the land.
- The survey helped to solve <u>future grievances</u> by providing <u>written evidence</u> of who all the land actually belonged to, rather than having to depend on people's <u>word</u>.

Military

- In <u>1085</u>, England was facing the threat of an <u>attack</u> by the <u>King of Denmark</u> and his <u>Norwegian</u> allies.
- In order to defend the country, the king needed to know what <u>military resources</u> were available to him. The survey provided vital information, like how many <u>knights</u> the king could summon to <u>fight</u> for him.

The Domesday Book

The Domesday Book was a massive undertaking and took a lot of organisation, but it was a very useful resource for ruling England. Test your knowledge of the Domesday Book with the activities on this page.

Knowledge and Understanding

1) In your own words, explain what the Domesday Book is.

2) Explain how the Anglo-Saxon system of government made it possible for the Normans to create the Domesday Book.

3) Why is the Domesday Book helpful for historians studying the Norman Conquest? Explain your answer.

4) Describe the role each of the following people played in the creation of the Domesday Book. Give as much detail as possible.

a) Tenants-in-chief   b) Commissioners   c) Juries

Interpretation

The interpretation below is about the uses of the Domesday Book.

> In 1085, William was having problems in England. His lords were arguing about land and he was facing the threat of a foreign attack. To solve these issues, he ordered a survey of England's land and resources, and his subjects around the country gathered information which was eventually compiled into the Great Domesday Book. This valuable resource aided the king in the defence of the country, gave him greater control over his income, and even helped him to settle those difficult arguments over land.

1) Explain whether the interpretation is convincing about the following subjects:

a) The problems England faced in 1085   b) Military uses of the Domesday Book   c) Legal uses of the Domesday Book   d) Financial uses of the Domesday Book

The Domesday Book — not as scary as it sounds...

It's important that you know about the Domesday Book and feel confident writing about it — make sure you can describe its features and explain why it was important to the Normans.

Life in Norman England

For peasants in English villages, life was more or less the same as it had been before the Norman Conquest.

England's Economy relied on Agriculture

1) The majority of people in Anglo-Saxon England were peasants or slaves. They lived in villages, which were governed by a thegn (see p.28). Farming was vital to the economy, so peasants and slaves mostly worked the land.

2) After 1066, English villages were mostly unchanged. The peasants who lived in them were still Anglo-Saxons, and their lives still revolved around farming their lord's land. The main difference was that their lord was likely to be a Norman rather than an Anglo-Saxon.

© Historic England / Mary Evans

3) Farming was hard work. There was no machinery, so almost everything was done by hand. Peasants would plough fields and plant seeds at the start of the year, before harvesting the crops in summer and autumn. Crops grown on a lord's land went straight to him, but most peasants also had their own land where they could grow food for themselves.

> This work was seasonal — it varied depending on the time of year and the weather.

4) Although most people were farmers, some villagers learnt a trade. For example, most villages needed a blacksmith (to make things out of iron) and a carpenter (to make things out of wood).

Village Life was Hard for Peasants

1) For the majority of peasants, living conditions were unpleasant and unhygienic. Their houses often only had one room where the whole family lived. There were no windows, and an open fire used for warmth and cooking made the house very smoky. The floor was made of earth with a layer of straw on top of it.

2) The food eaten by peasants varied depending on what they could grow or catch themselves. The main crops grown in the fields were wheat, rye and barley, which could be used to make bread. Peasants might grow fruit and vegetables on their own plots of land, and keep animals to give them access to eggs, milk and cheese. They might also hunt in forests and fish in nearby rivers.

> The introduction of forest law (see p.34) made life even more difficult for the peasants — it limited the land that was available for hunting, fishing, gathering food or collecting firewood.

3) If there was a bad harvest or the peasants' crops were destroyed by animals or the weather, they would go hungry or even starve.

Comment and Analysis

Peasants' lives were very different from those of the rich, who were able to afford a higher standard of living. For example, meat was very expensive, so most peasants couldn't afford to eat it, but the rich ate a lot of it. The rich avoided eating fruit, vegetables and dairy simply because these foods were associated with the poor.

The Normans Rebuilt some Anglo-Saxon Buildings

1) Villages were in rural locations — they were surrounded by the fields where villagers grew crops. As well as the peasants' houses, there would usually be a church and a manor house for the lord.

2) In Anglo-Saxon England, buildings were usually made from wood or wattle and daub (wooden strips that were stuck together with materials such as clay, soil and manure).

3) The Normans often rebuilt important buildings, such as churches and manor houses, in stone. They might also construct new buildings. For example, in Wharram Percy, a village in Yorkshire, the Normans built a stone mill for grinding grain to make flour.

Life in Norman England

The majority of the population in Norman England was made up of peasants who lived in villages. Have a go at the activities on this page to make sure you understand what life in the villages was like.

Knowledge and Understanding

1) Copy and complete the diagram below, giving details about the work peasants did at different times of the year.

a) Start of the year: ⟶ b) Summer and autumn:

2) Give two jobs that villagers did in Norman England, other than farming.

3) Copy and complete the mind map below, giving information about what peasants' houses were like in Norman England.

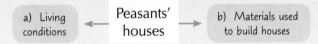

a) Living conditions ⟵ Peasants' houses ⟶ b) Materials used to build houses

4) Describe the location of villages in Norman England.

5) Which buildings might have been made of stone in English villages after the conquest?

Thinking Historically

1) How much did the Norman Conquest affect the following aspects of village life? Explain your answers.

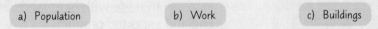

a) Population   b) Work   c) Buildings

2) Copy and complete the mind map below, explaining how each of the factors in the green boxes affected the type of food people ate. You should give examples of food in your answers.

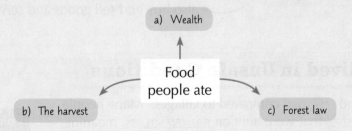

a) Wealth

Food people ate

b) The harvest   c) Forest law

Village life — it was unpleasant to be a peasant...

Think about how changes made by the Normans affected people at different levels of society. For example, forest law set aside land for the king to hunt in, but it impacted peasants' lives too.

Life Under the Normans

Life in Norman England

The Normans brought <u>major changes</u> to English towns — some <u>destruction</u> followed by a lot of <u>development</u>.

More People started living in Towns after 1066

1) There weren't a lot of towns in Anglo-Saxon England, and most of them were quite small. Many towns were seriously affected by the <u>conquest</u> and the <u>rebellions</u> that followed — <u>buildings</u> were <u>destroyed</u> and the <u>local economy</u> was <u>badly damaged</u>.

2) However, the towns began to <u>recover</u> in the years following the Norman Conquest:

- Under the Normans, towns played a more important role in <u>society</u> and the <u>economy</u> than in Anglo-Saxon England — they were centres of <u>administration</u> and <u>trade</u>. They also had <u>military</u> and <u>religious</u> functions, as the Normans built lots of <u>castles</u>, <u>churches</u> and <u>cathedrals</u> in towns.

- As people started to move to towns from rural areas, some <u>existing towns</u> grew (e.g. Nottingham) and some <u>new towns</u> developed (e.g. St Albans). Some of the <u>largest</u> and <u>wealthiest towns</u> attracted <u>immigrants</u> from <u>abroad</u> (e.g. Canterbury).

- These developments helped the <u>economy</u> of towns by creating <u>demand</u> for <u>goods and services</u>. For example, the construction of new buildings made work for <u>craftsmen</u> (see below) like carpenters and stone masons.

> Even though <u>more people</u> started living in <u>towns</u> after 1066, <u>most people</u> still lived in <u>villages</u> (see p.38).

There was a Wide Range of Different Jobs

1) Unlike in villages (see p.38), where most people worked the land, people did a <u>wide variety</u> of <u>jobs</u> in towns. Some people worked as <u>servants</u> for the rich inhabitants of the town, whereas others learnt a <u>trade</u> and became <u>craftsmen</u>.

2) Craftsmen were important to a town's <u>economy</u>, as they produced <u>goods</u> that could be <u>bought</u> and <u>sold</u>. They started as <u>apprentices</u> and worked for a <u>master craftsman</u> to learn the skills of their trade, before <u>leaving</u> their master and <u>earning money</u> themselves. There were lots of different craftsmen in towns, such as <u>butchers</u>, <u>bakers</u>, <u>tailors</u>, <u>shoemakers</u>, <u>carpenters</u> and <u>stone masons</u>.

> The <u>feudal system</u> (see p.28) is a <u>simple version</u> of the <u>social structure</u> of Norman England — in reality, it was <u>more complicated</u>. The inhabitants of towns are an example of a group that didn't really fit into the feudal system.

> While people in <u>rural areas</u> could <u>grow crops</u> and <u>keep animals</u>, people living in towns were more likely to <u>buy</u> their food at <u>markets</u>. However, it was <u>very difficult</u> to keep food <u>fresh</u> during the 11th century. Meat might be <u>preserved</u> by <u>salting</u> it or <u>smoking</u> it. Sometimes <u>rotten meat</u> might have <u>spices</u> added in order to hide the taste.

3) <u>Merchants</u> also worked in towns. The <u>conquest</u> caused an increase in <u>trade</u> with <u>Normandy</u> and the rest of <u>France</u> — England <u>exported</u> products such as <u>wool</u> to other countries and <u>imported</u> goods from abroad such as <u>wine</u> and <u>textiles</u>. Many merchants became <u>very wealthy</u> as a result.

4) Many craftsmen and merchants worked on the <u>high street</u>, which was the <u>main road</u> through the town. People could also buy and sell goods and services in the <u>market square</u>.

Townspeople lived in Unsafe Conditions

1) Towns were <u>busy</u> and <u>crowded</u> compared to villages. Many people lived in <u>wooden houses</u> that were built on <u>narrow streets</u>, meaning <u>living conditions</u> were often <u>cramped</u> and <u>unhygienic</u>. <u>Fire</u> was also a risk as it could <u>spread easily</u> between the houses.

2) Conditions in towns could be <u>even more unhealthy</u> than in villages. As towns had larger populations, <u>rubbish</u> and <u>waste</u> could build up more quickly. This meant that <u>disease</u> was common in towns.

Comment and Analysis

In Norman England, the risk of things like <u>starvation</u> and <u>disease</u> meant that the average <u>life expectancy</u> for ordinary people was <u>very low</u>.

Life Under the Normans

Life in Norman England

There were more opportunities for people in towns than for people in villages, but there were problems with life in towns as well. Try the activities below to check that you know all about towns in Norman England.

Knowledge and Understanding

1) Copy and complete the mind map below, explaining the different ways that towns changed between Anglo-Saxon England and Norman England. Give as much detail as possible.

Ways towns changed

2) Describe how people trained to become craftsmen.

3) Give two places in a town where people would buy and sell goods and services.

4) Give three differences between villages and towns in Norman England.

Interpretation

The interpretation below describes what towns were like in Norman England.

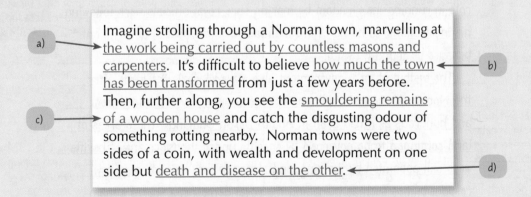

a) → the work being carried out by countless masons and carpenters.

Imagine strolling through a Norman town, marvelling at the work being carried out by countless masons and carpenters. It's difficult to believe how much the town has been transformed from just a few years before. Then, further along, you see the smouldering remains of a wooden house and catch the disgusting odour of something rotting nearby. Norman towns were two sides of a coin, with wealth and development on one side but death and disease on the other.

b) → how much the town has been transformed

c) → smouldering remains of a wooden house

d) → death and disease on the other

1) Explain whether you find each of the highlighted phrases above convincing about what towns were like in Norman England.

Towns eventually profited from the Norman Conquest...

In the exam, you only have a limited amount of time to answer each question. If you're spending too long on one question, write a conclusion then move on to the next question.

Worked Exam-Style Question

This worked answer will help you with the question where you need to give an account of an event or development in Norman England. Remember to discuss and analyse a range of features for this question.

Give an account of how the system of government
stayed the same after the Norman Conquest.   [8 marks]

The first sentence addresses the question.

Many things about the system of government remained the same after the Norman Conquest, such as the structure of the government. In Anglo-Saxon England, the government was centralised, with power focused around the king. Although William filled his government with Normans rather than Anglo-Saxons, he kept the existing centralised structure. This is because it made him the most powerful person in the government, which helped him to maintain control of the country. Another aspect of William's government was that he used a council to help him govern the kingdom, just as Anglo-Saxon kings had been assisted by the Witan. This council was called the Curia Regis and was made up of tenants-in-chief who advised the king.

This describes a feature of the government that stayed the same and analyses its effect.

The answer looks at how multiple features of the system of government stayed the same after the conquest.

Some aspects of the system of government stayed the same because William adopted features of the Anglo-Saxon system that had not existed in Normandy. For example, he used writs, which were short documents containing royal commands for local government officials to follow. Although writs were a common feature of the Anglo-Saxon government, they were a new tool for William. Writs helped him to take a more direct role in running the kingdom by making sure royal officials were following his instructions, so he may have maintained this aspect of government because he found it useful.

The explanation links the point back to the question.

The system of local government also stayed largely the same after the Norman Conquest. William kept the country divided into shires and hundreds as it had been in Anglo-Saxon England. These areas of land continued to be governed by sheriffs under the Normans. Sheriffs were still appointed by the king, and although they gained some new responsibilities such as managing the royal demesne, a sheriff's main duties remained the same as they had been in Anglo-Saxon England. Sheriffs still supervised the collection of fines and taxes, judged civil and criminal cases in local courts and organised military forces. Earls also performed some of these duties and continued to play an important role in helping the king run the country, although they were less powerful than the Anglo-Saxon earls had been. Maintaining these aspects of local government ensured that William had effective support in running the whole of the country.

Specific details show good knowledge of the period.

Exam-Style Questions

Use your knowledge of what life was like under the Normans to help you answer these exam-style questions.

Interpretation 1

This interpretation shows an artist's impression of village life in Norman England.

Exam-Style Questions

1) To what extent is Interpretation 1 convincing about villages in Norman England?
   Use Interpretation 1 and your own knowledge to explain your answer.   [8 marks]

2) How were towns important in Norman England? Explain your answer.   [8 marks]

3) Give an account of the ways that the legal
   system changed after the Norman Conquest.   [8 marks]

The Anglo-Saxon Church

The Church was an important part of people's lives in Anglo-Saxon England, affecting everyone from peasants to nobles to kings. Unfortunately, there were lots of problems in the Church — it was pretty far from perfect...

The Church was an Important Part of Everyday Life

1) Before 1066, the Church played an important role in Anglo-Saxon society and its influence over ordinary people was already growing.

2) The Anglo-Saxon Church was split up into sixteen large areas called dioceses, each one controlled by a bishop. By 1066, these regions were starting to be divided into smaller areas called parishes.

3) Each parish was based around a local community, so the Church became more involved in ordinary people's lives.

4) Parish churches were built in towns and villages — each church had a priest to look after the people in the parish.

> The priest said mass regularly and performed key ceremonies such as baptism and burial. He also got people to confess their sins and do penance (show that they're sorry for their sins).

The Church and the Nobility had an Important Relationship

1) The Church held influence over the nobility, as well as over ordinary people.

2) The king and his nobles gave churches gifts of land and precious objects, and helped to protect them from violence and robbery. This was called patronage.

3) The nobility sometimes sent their second-born sons to train as priests, which helped the Church to grow. This also reduced competition for land within the nobility by giving some men a job within the Church.

4) Nobles tried to control the appointment of churchmen so they could give the most valuable, influential posts to their relatives or followers.

5) In return, churchmen prayed for their patrons. Prayer was important to the nobility, because they believed that it would give them success on earth and help them to get into heaven.

6) Even the king needed the Church's support to legitimise his claim to power — people thought that a ruler needed God's support to be successful. If the Church supported him, it was seen as a sign that God was on his side.

Comment and Analysis

The sources produced by churchmen were often influenced by the relationship between the Church and the nobility — for example, this image shows King Cnut (a Danish king who ruled England in the early 11th century) being crowned by an angel. It was created by the monks of Winchester, who were close to the king. It makes his claim to the throne seem more legitimate (valid), as it implies that God wants him to be king.

There were Lots of Problems within the Church

1) Corruption was common in the Anglo-Saxon Church. Many churchmen took advantage of their position and broke religious law. Some of the Church's main problems included:

- Pluralism — Churchmen were forbidden from holding multiple religious offices (roles within the Church), but some held more than one at a time.
- Simony — Some churchmen bought and sold religious offices and promotions.
- Nepotism — Some churchmen gave religious offices to their friends or relatives.
- Clerical Marriage — Churchmen were meant to remain unmarried and dedicate their lives to God, but a lot of Anglo-Saxon churchmen had wives or mistresses.

2) Some of the most powerful figures in the Anglo-Saxon Church were guilty of corruption, such as Archbishop Stigand of Canterbury. Stigand committed pluralism by continuing to hold the position of Bishop of Winchester after becoming Archbishop of Canterbury.

The Anglo-Saxon Church

Although the Anglo-Saxon Church was corrupt, it had a great deal of influence in people's lives.
The activities on this page will help you to practise what you've learnt about the Anglo-Saxon Church.

Knowledge and Understanding

1) Using the key words below, explain how the Anglo-Saxon Church was structured.

dioceses   parishes   bishop

2) Give two examples of how the Church was involved in ordinary people's lives.

3) Copy and complete the table below, giving a definition
for each problem in the Anglo-Saxon Church.

Problem	Definition
a) Pluralism	
b) Simony	
c) Nepotism	
d) Clerical Marriage	

4) Explain how Stigand contributed to corruption in the Anglo-Saxon Church.

Thinking Historically

1) Copy and complete the mind maps below, giving as many ways as possible that
the Church and the nobility benefited from their relationship with each other.

← Church →   ← Nobility →

2) Why was it important for the king to have a good
relationship with the Church? Explain your answer.

Pluralism is writing churchmans instead of churchmen...

*It's really important to understand change and continuity during the period you're studying.
By learning about the Anglo-Saxon Church, you'll be able to compare it to the Norman Church.*

Norman Church Reform

The Church was still very important <u>after the conquest</u> — it had a lot of <u>power</u> and <u>influence</u>. The Normans made a few <u>changes</u> to its <u>organisation</u>, as well as to the <u>churchmen</u> running it.

The Norman Church had a Strict Hierarchy

1) The <u>Archbishop of Canterbury</u> was the most important person in the Norman Church (see p.48). There was also an <u>Archbishop of York</u>, but he didn't have as much power.

2) Below the archbishops, the Church was divided into <u>dioceses</u> (see p.44). This was the same as it had been in Anglo-Saxon England, but the Normans <u>reorganised</u> certain dioceses by moving the <u>headquarters</u> from <u>rural areas</u> or <u>small towns</u> (e.g. Dorchester) to <u>larger towns</u> (e.g. Lincoln).

3) Dioceses were divided into smaller areas called <u>archdeaconries</u>, which were divided again into <u>deaneries</u> and <u>parishes</u>. These were all controlled by <u>different churchmen</u>:

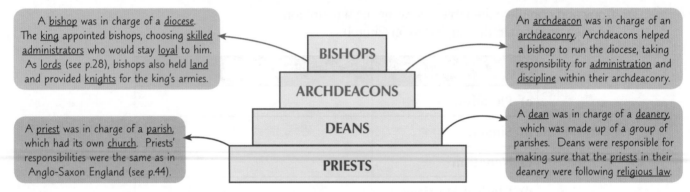

A <u>bishop</u> was in charge of a <u>diocese</u>. The <u>king</u> appointed bishops, choosing <u>skilled administrators</u> who would stay <u>loyal</u> to him. As <u>lords</u> (see p.28), bishops also held <u>land</u> and provided <u>knights</u> for the king's armies.

An <u>archdeacon</u> was in charge of an <u>archdeaconry</u>. Archdeacons helped a bishop to run the diocese, taking responsibility for <u>administration</u> and <u>discipline</u> within their archdeaconry.

BISHOPS
ARCHDEACONS
DEANS
PRIESTS

A <u>priest</u> was in charge of a <u>parish</u>, which had its own <u>church</u>. Priests' responsibilities were the same as in Anglo-Saxon England (see p.44).

A <u>dean</u> was in charge of a <u>deanery</u>, which was made up of a group of parishes. Deans were responsible for making sure that the <u>priests</u> in their deanery were following <u>religious law</u>.

4) These roles had all existed in the <u>Anglo-Saxon Church</u>, but the Normans <u>changed</u> some of them slightly. Before 1066, for example, <u>archdeacons</u> helped bishops to run the dioceses without taking responsibility for a <u>particular region</u>. The creation of <u>archdeaconries</u> under the Normans made them more <u>influential</u>.

William I Replaced Anglo-Saxon Church Leaders

1) William I <u>replaced</u> the <u>most powerful figures</u> in the English Church (e.g. <u>archbishops</u> and <u>bishops</u>) with his own <u>supporters</u>. Some Anglo-Saxon churchmen were <u>forced</u> to leave their posts, but William waited for others to <u>step down</u> before replacing them. By <u>1087</u>, only <u>one</u> bishop in England was <u>Anglo-Saxon</u>.

2) The most significant replacement was Stigand, the Anglo-Saxon <u>Archbishop of Canterbury</u> — in <u>1070</u>, William decided to replace him with an Italian supporter called <u>Lanfranc</u> (see p.48)

3) However, William didn't replace Anglo-Saxon churchmen at <u>lower levels</u>. There were lots of Anglo-Saxon <u>monks</u> in Norman England, and the majority of <u>priests</u> were also Anglo-Saxons.

Comment and Analysis

William I needed the <u>support</u> of churchmen because they were <u>powerful</u> figures in <u>society</u>. They held large amounts of <u>land</u> and played a vital role in <u>government</u>. They were also able to <u>influence</u> ordinary people's <u>opinions</u> about the conquest, as well as their <u>attitudes</u> towards the Normans.

The Church had its own Justice System

1) Before 1066, a <u>churchman</u> who had been accused of a <u>crime</u> would be tried in a <u>secular</u> (non-religious) court.

See p.34 for more on secular courts.

2) Lanfranc introduced <u>church courts</u> to enforce <u>religious law</u>. This meant that churchmen were no longer tried in the <u>hundred courts</u>, and so were tried <u>separately</u> from lay people. Some churchmen could still appear in the <u>shire courts</u>, but it happened much <u>less often</u>.

3) The church courts were meant to <u>avoid secular interference</u>, but the king could still <u>overrule</u> their <u>decisions</u>. This sometimes caused <u>conflict</u> between the <u>king</u> and the <u>Church</u> (see p.52).

Norman Church Reform

Complete these activities to make sure you understand how the Normans affected the English Church.

Knowledge and Understanding

The diagram below shows the Church hierarchy in Norman England.

1) Copy and complete the diagram, filling in the type of churchmen at each level in the Church hierarchy and adding as much extra information about them as you can.

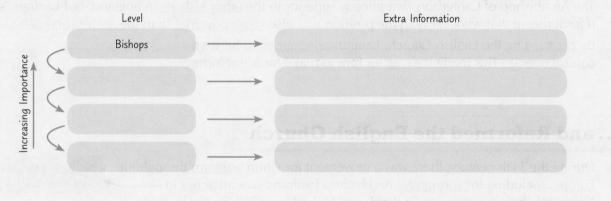

Level — Bishops

Extra Information

Increasing Importance

Thinking Historically

1) Why was it important for the Normans to have control over the Church?

2) Copy and complete the table below, explaining whether there was change or continuity in each aspect of the Church between Anglo-Saxon England and Norman England.

Aspect of the Church	Change or continuity?	Explanation for choice
a) Structure of dioceses		
b) Churchmen at the top of the Church hierarchy		
c) Churchmen at lower levels of the Church hierarchy		
d) How churchmen were tried for crimes		

William I really made his mark on the Church...

It's important that you can use language to link an event to its causes and consequences — linking words and phrases like 'as a result', 'despite this', and 'therefore' can help you do this.

Norman Church Reform

Some of the most important changes to the English Church were made by Archbishop Lanfranc, one of William I's closest advisors. Lanfranc was full of ideas to reform the Church and solve its problems.

Archbishop Lanfranc established the Primacy of Canterbury...

1) After becoming archbishop in 1070, Lanfranc made the Norman Church more centralised (controlled by a single authority). With the support of the king, he made the Archbishop of Canterbury the primate of England.

> The 'primate' is the most important churchman in a particular region.

2) The Archbishop of Canterbury was already superior to the other bishops in England, but Lanfranc's reform meant that whoever held the position was also more powerful than the Archbishop of York.

3) By centralising the English Church, Lanfranc strengthened his own control over it. This made it easier for him to make further reforms.

... and Reformed the English Church

1) During the 11th century, there was a movement for Church reform throughout Europe, including in Normandy. Archbishop Lanfranc was an abbot in Normandy before coming to England, and he had been influenced by these Church reforms. He wanted to carry out similar reforms in the English Church.

> An abbot is the chief monk in a monastery (see p.54).

2) Lanfranc used councils to impose discipline on the Church. At these councils, churchmen discussed different aspects of religious law and made important decisions about how to tackle the Church's problems.

3) Lanfranc also brought church courts to England (see p.46) in order to try churchmen who had been accused of breaking religious law. This gave the Church more control over how churchmen were disciplined.

Lanfranc's reforms allowed him to enforce stricter rules for how all churchmen should behave — he used them to tackle problems like pluralism, simony, nepotism and clerical marriage (see p.44).

Comment and Analysis

Some of these changes had started to affect the English Church before 1066, but the Norman Conquest might have increased the speed of change by introducing new churchmen to England who were keen on reform.

The Normans built Churches and Cathedrals

1) As well as reforming the English Church, the Normans started a church-building programme — within fifty years of the invasion, work had begun on rebuilding almost all major churches in England, and many parish churches were also rebuilt.

2) The Normans built churches, cathedrals and monasteries in the Romanesque style of architecture that was popular in Western Europe. This meant that they were inspired by Roman buildings and included details such as high arches and wide columns.

> A cathedral is the most important church in a diocese. It's where the bishop is based.

Durham Cathedral is an example of a church that was rebuilt using the Romanesque style.

3) The Normans believed supporting the Church was a way of serving God. The churches also served as a visible and permanent symbol of the Normans' dominance over England. This reinforced the authority of the Normans in a similar way to castles (see p.14-16).

4) As well as building churches, the Normans also granted land to the Church — by 1086, the Church held around a quarter of the land in England. This meant that senior churchmen such as archbishops, bishops and abbots were among the most important lords in the country, with access to a lot of power and wealth.

The Norman Church and Monasticism

Norman Church Reform

The appointment of Lanfranc as Archbishop of Canterbury after the Norman Conquest led to lots of changes in the English Church. Complete the activities below to help you understand these changes.

Knowledge and Understanding

1) Using the key words below, explain what the Primacy of Canterbury is.

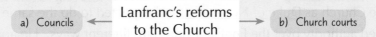

| England | Archbishop of Canterbury | Archbishop of York | primate |

2) Copy and complete the mind map below by adding information about how Lanfranc used councils and church courts to reform the English Church.

a) Councils ← Lanfranc's reforms to the Church → b) Church courts

3) Why might the Norman Conquest have sped up the process of Church reform in England?

4) Explain how the Norman Conquest affected religious buildings in England.

5) Why did the Normans support the Church?

Thinking Historically

1) In your own words, explain how establishing the Primacy of Canterbury helped Lanfranc to reform the Church.

2) Copy and complete the mind map below by adding information under each heading about why Norman Church reform was important. Use the information on pages 46 and 48 to help you.

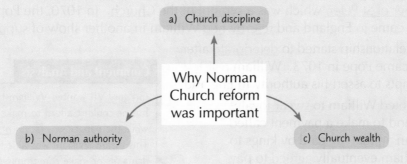

a) Church discipline

Why Norman Church reform was important

b) Norman authority

c) Church wealth

The new Archbishop was Lanfranc about changes...

If you get a question about developments in the Church in the exam, there are lots of different aspects you could write about, from Lanfranc's reforms to changes to the Church's structure.

William I and the Church

William I was a very religious king, but that doesn't necessarily mean he always got on well with the Church.

William I wanted to Limit the Church's Power

1) William I was very religious. He made large donations to churches and cathedrals and oversaw the construction of new monasteries. He was also very supportive of the idea of reform (see p.48). This helped William to build a strong relationship with the Church.

2) After the upheaval of the Norman Conquest, William I's relations with the English Church were particularly important. The Church was influential and William needed its support to help him establish control over the kingdom.

> The need to maintain good relations with the Church helps to explain why William didn't replace Archbishop Stigand until 1070 (see p.46). Stigand was too powerful to remove until England was more secure, and William could also use him to negotiate with the Anglo-Saxons.

3) However, William wasn't willing to let the Church interfere in running the kingdom. He had been able to control the Church as Duke of Normandy and expected to do the same as King of England.

4) William maintained authority over the English Church in different ways. He appointed churchmen who were loyal to him and reserved the right to overrule important decisions which were made in church councils or courts. He also took control of communication between England and the Pope.

The Pope wanted to Assert Authority in Europe

1) The Pope was the leader of the Church in Western Europe. This made him an extremely powerful figure.

2) During the late 11th century, a Pope called Gregory VII and his successors started to push for the Church to become free from secular influence. However, this caused problems like the Investiture Controversy:

- Pope Gregory VII wanted to prevent rulers from choosing bishops and abbots. He believed they should be chosen by the Church.
- This caused conflict with rulers in England, France and Germany, who all wanted to maintain control over the Church in their own countries.
- This conflict was a massive threat to the papacy's authority — in 1080, Henry IV of Germany tried to remove Gregory VII as Pope.

> 'Investiture' refers to the appointment of bishops and abbots.

> The office of the Pope is known as the papacy.

William I had an Uneasy Relationship with the Pope

1) At the time of the Norman Conquest, William had a good relationship with the papacy. Pope Alexander II supported William's invasion of England and allowed him to march under the Banner of St Peter, which was a symbol of the Church. In 1070, the Pope's representatives came to England and re-crowned William in another show of support.

2) However, this relationship started to deteriorate after Gregory VII became Pope in 1073. William resisted Gregory's attempts to assert his authority in England.

3) Gregory VII wanted William to swear loyalty to the papacy and to make a payment called Peter's Pence (an annual tax paid by kings to the Pope). William eventually agreed to pay the tax, but he refused to swear loyalty.

> **Comment and Analysis**
>
> Gregory VII wanted William to recognise his authority, but he couldn't afford to make another powerful enemy while the papacy was facing other problems (see above). This meant William was able to ignore some of the Pope's demands or make compromises that were beneficial to him.

4) William wouldn't allow the papacy to influence the appointment of bishops and abbots in England (see above). He wanted to be able to appoint churchmen who he could trust to remain loyal to him.

5) Archbishop Lanfranc also had an uneasy relationship with the Pope. Gregory VII strongly objected to the Primacy of Canterbury (see p.48) and refused to recognise Lanfranc's increased authority unless he went to Rome and submitted to the Pope. He summoned Lanfranc multiple times, but Lanfranc refused to go.

William I and the Church

Try these activities to test your knowledge of William I's relationship with the Church and the papacy.

Knowledge and Understanding

1) Explain how William I built a strong relationship with the Church.

2) Give two reasons why William didn't replace Stigand as Archbishop of Canterbury until 1070.

3) Write a definition for the following terms:
   a) Pope
   b) Papacy
   c) Investiture

4) Explain what caused the Investiture Controversy.

5) Describe William's relationship with Pope Alexander II.

6) Why did Archbishop Lanfranc and Pope Gregory VII have an uneasy relationship?

Thinking Historically

1) Copy and complete the mind map below by adding the different ways that William I kept control of the Church.

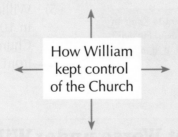

How William kept control of the Church

2) Why was the Investiture Controversy important for each of the following? Explain your answer.

a) William's relationship with the Pope

b) William's authority in England

EXAM TIP

Gregory wasn't everyone's favourite Pope...

William dealt with a lot of important people while trying to gain control of the Church.
Make sure you know who these people were and whether they supported or opposed William.

William II and the Church

If you thought that William I had an uneasy relationship with the Church, just wait until you meet William II...

William II used the Church for Personal Gain...

1) According to several sources from the time, William II wasn't as religious as his father. He used the Church to make money, which made him unpopular with many churchmen.

Comment and Analysis

William II's poor relationship with the Church means many of the sources about him are biased, as they were written by monks who disliked him — this makes it difficult for historians to know what William II was really like.

2) William made money by delaying the appointment of senior churchmen like archbishops, bishops and abbots. This allowed him to take all of the income that these churchmen would have received.

3) When Lanfranc died in 1089, William didn't appoint another Archbishop of Canterbury until 1093. He took the archbishop's income for four years, and only appointed a new one (Anselm) after falling seriously ill. He believed that God would punish him if he died while the position was still vacant.

... and tried to Control the Church

1) Like William I, William II was determined to assert royal authority over the Church from the start of his reign. In 1088, he proved his authority during the trial of William of Saint-Calais, the Bishop of Durham, who had taken part in Odo of Bayeux's rebellion against the new king (see p.24).

2) William of Saint-Calais wanted to be tried in a church court, but the king insisted on the trial taking place in the king's court (see p.34). William of Saint-Calais didn't attend the trial, but his land was taken from him after other bishops and nobles decided to support the king.

This case caused conflict with the Pope, who supported William of Saint-Calais and asked for his lands to be restored. William II ignored the Pope's request.

3) However, William II wasn't always able to control the Church. In the 1090s, he came into conflict with Archbishop Anselm of Canterbury. The two men disagreed about England's relationship with the papacy.

4) William thought that Anselm's ultimate loyalty should be to the king, but Anselm believed that his loyalty to the Pope was more important. At the Council of Rockingham in 1095, a group of bishops and nobles told Anselm to obey the king, but he refused. This created a lot of tension between William and Anselm.

Anselm was so frustrated that he went to Rome to seek support from the Pope (see below). He didn't return to England until after William died in 1100.

5) William and Anselm came into conflict again in 1097 because the king refused to allow the Church to hold councils. This stopped Anselm from making important changes to the Church.

Papal Relations got a lot Worse under William II

1) For most of William II's reign, there were two rival claimants to the papacy (Urban II and Clement III).

2) William refused to support either Urban or Clement. He wanted to take advantage of the division in the papacy and strengthen his own position by not acknowledging either claimant. This caused conflict with Archbishop Anselm (see above), who had acknowledged Urban II as the rightful Pope.

3) William II eventually acknowledged Urban II in 1095, after Urban agreed not to send representatives or letters to England without the king's permission — this let William limit the Pope's influence in England.

4) However, England's relations with the papacy deteriorated after William and Anselm came into conflict over church councils in 1097 (see above). Urban II showed support for Anselm by threatening the king with excommunication (exclusion from the Church). This was the most severe form of religious penalty.

William II and the Church

William II wanted to control the Church and make money from it. However, this didn't make him very popular. Try these activities to make sure you understand William II's relationship with the Church.

Knowledge and Understanding

1) Why is it difficult to know what William II was really like?

2) How did William use the Church to make money?

3) Copy and complete the timeline below by filling in the key events of William's relationship with the Church and the papacy. Give as much detail as possible for each date.

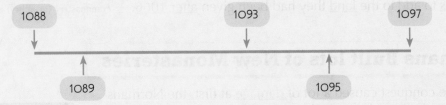

4) Explain how the trial of William of Saint-Calais showed William II's authority over the Church.

5) Why was the division in the papacy useful to William?

Interpretation

The interpretation below is about William II and Archbishop Anselm.

> Try as he might, William couldn't compel Anselm to show the kind of loyalty the king felt he deserved. Even at the demand of the king's leading nobles and bishops to pledge himself wholly to William, the Archbishop would not compromise on his devotion to Rome. In the face of William's hostility, Anselm turned to the Pope, who threatened William with greater force than Anselm could muster on his own.

1) Explain whether the interpretation is convincing about the following subjects:

| a) William's relationship with Anselm | b) William's relationship with English bishops | c) William's relationship with the Pope |

William II wanted a rich, religious experience...

When you answer the interpretation question, you should bring in relevant knowledge to back up your points. Make sure you link this knowledge to the information in the interpretation.

Norman Monasticism

Worshipping God was important in the 11th century, and some people made it into a full-time job by becoming monks. The Norman Conquest led to lots of changes for the monasteries in England.

Anglo-Saxon Monasteries were Damaged by the Conquest

1) Before 1066, there were lots of abbeys and monasteries in England. They became wealthy and powerful during the 10th and 11th centuries due to the support of kings and the nobility, who gave them valuable gifts and land.

2) The Norman Conquest had a devastating impact on the monasteries. They were an easy target for the Normans, who took their land and wealth. Some of the land was given to monasteries in Normandy, but the majority of it was claimed by secular lords to add to the land they had been given after 1066.

A monastery (or abbey) is a place occupied by monks.

The Normans Built lots of New Monasteries

1) Although the conquest caused a lot of damage at first, the Normans soon started to build and restore abbeys and monasteries in England.

2) For example, William I founded Battle Abbey on the site of the Battle of Hastings. The Norman nobility also founded abbeys and monasteries — Roger of Montgomery, who William I appointed as Earl of Shrewsbury after the invasion, founded Shrewsbury Abbey on the site of an Anglo-Saxon church in 1083.

3) Many abbeys and monasteries in northern England had been abandoned due to Viking raids between the 8th and 10th centuries. The Normans refounded some of these, such as Whitby Abbey, which was refounded in about 1078.

Comment and Analysis

The Normans were worried that God would punish them for the violence of the conquest, and thought building monasteries would help them to earn forgiveness. Battle Abbey might also have been built as a symbol of William's victory over Harold.

The Normans helped to Revive Monastic Life in England

1) Before 1066, all monks in England followed the Rule of St Benedict. However, monasteries interpreted the Rule differently and operated differently as a result.

2) In the 11th century, a group of monks from the Abbey of Cluny in France (Cluniacs) started to reform and reorganise monasteries across Europe. They wanted monks to follow the Rule of St Benedict more strictly.

3) The Norman Conquest helped these monastic reforms to take place in England:

- Monasteries in Normandy had already been affected by the Cluniacs' reforms, and the Normans brought these ideas to England after 1066.
- William I replaced most Anglo-Saxon abbots with Normans, including at Peterborough, Glastonbury and Winchester. These new abbots might have been more open to reform.
- Ordinary monks also helped to encourage reform. The Normans didn't get rid of Anglo-Saxon monks, but a lot of monks came from Normandy, particularly to join new monasteries.

4) The Normans' openness to reform encouraged different groups of monks to found monasteries in England. The Cluniacs arrived in England in the late 1070s, and William de Warenne founded a Cluniac monastery at Lewes not long afterwards. By 1100, England had many more Cluniac monasteries.

5) Other monks such as the Augustinians followed later. The Augustinians lived a different lifestyle from the Benedictines — they followed the Rule of St Augustine instead of the Rule of St Benedict. Augustinian monasteries were founded at Canterbury, Colchester and Huntingdon in the 1090s.

Norman Monasticism

The Normans built lots of new monasteries and had a major impact on monastic life after the conquest. Give these activities a go to see if you understand how monasticism developed in Norman England.

Knowledge and Understanding

1) Using the key words below, explain what Anglo-Saxon monasteries were like before the conquest.

land   Rule   support

2) Explain how Anglo-Saxon monasteries were damaged as a result of the conquest.

3) Copy and complete the table below, giving as much detail as you can about the construction of each abbey.

Abbey	Details of its construction
a) Battle Abbey	
b) Shrewsbury Abbey	
c) Whitby Abbey	

4) Why did the Normans build monasteries after the conquest?

5) Give as much information as you can about each of the following groups of monks:
a) the Cluniacs
b) the Augustinians

Thinking Historically

1) Copy and complete the mind map below, explaining how the Normans affected each aspect of monastic life.

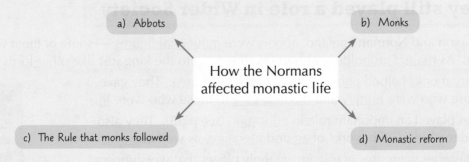

a) Abbots   b) Monks

How the Normans affected monastic life

c) The Rule that monks followed   d) Monastic reform

The Normans were blessed with reforming monks...

When answering a question, introduce each new point by linking it to what the question is asking — this will keep you on track and show the examiner why your points are relevant.

Life in a Norman Monastery

The lives of <u>monks</u> in Norman England involved lots of <u>praying</u>, <u>reading</u>, <u>writing</u> and waking up far too early.

Norman Monasteries were built with a Standard Layout

1) Most Norman monasteries were made up of a <u>single church</u> with a <u>cloister</u> attached to it.

2) The <u>cloister</u> was an important part of a monastery. It was often designed to allow <u>sunlight</u> in so that it could be used as a <u>scriptorium</u> (a place for the monks to <u>read</u> and <u>write</u>). Monks could also <u>meditate</u> in the cloister, and it was used for <u>religious processions</u>.

3) Other important buildings in a monastery included the <u>dormitory</u> (where the monks <u>slept</u>), the <u>refectory</u> (where they had <u>meals</u>) and the <u>chapter house</u> (where they had <u>meetings</u>). The Normans usually built these from <u>stone</u>, whereas the Anglo-Saxons often built them from <u>wood</u>.

4) Monasteries looked different depending on the monks living in them. The <u>Cluniacs</u> (see p.54) used <u>elaborate decorations</u>, while other monasteries were quite <u>plain</u>. Some Anglo-Saxon monasteries had used decorations (e.g. <u>stained glass</u>), but it was only the <u>richest</u> ones.

> Anglo-Saxon monasteries <u>varied</u> in <u>layout</u> and often had <u>multiple churches</u>. Some of them might have had <u>cloisters</u>, but these were only a <u>regular feature</u> in monasteries after the Norman Conquest.

> The <u>cloister</u> was made up of four <u>covered walkways</u> surrounding a <u>courtyard</u>.

Monks Lived Separately from Other People...

1) Monasteries allowed monks to live <u>away</u> from <u>lay people</u> and the <u>distractions</u> of <u>ordinary life</u>. This was supposed to help them to <u>devote</u> their lives to <u>God</u>.

2) Different groups of monks (see p.54) lived <u>different lifestyles</u>. The <u>Benedictines</u> lived in the following way:

- Monks <u>woke up early</u> in the morning (at around <u>two o'clock</u>) for the <u>first service</u> of the day. The <u>final service</u> might take place at around <u>seven o'clock</u> in the evening.

- They attended <u>eight services</u> a day, which were often performed in <u>Latin</u>. The monks <u>prayed</u> and sang or chanted <u>religious songs</u>.

- Between services, the monks had work to do — some tasks were essential to the running of the monastery (e.g. <u>managing supplies</u>), but monks also spent a lot of time <u>reading</u> and <u>writing</u> (see p.58).

- The monks ate <u>two meals</u> a day, and they weren't allowed to eat <u>meat</u> as it was a <u>luxury</u>.

- Monks were <u>discouraged</u> from talking during the <u>day</u> and <u>forbidden</u> from talking at <u>night</u>.

> The <u>content</u> of these services <u>changed</u> under the Normans. In 1083, a group of Anglo-Saxon monks at Glastonbury Abbey <u>rebelled</u> against the new abbot after the <u>introduction</u> of <u>new practices</u>.

... but they still played a role in Wider Society

1) In Anglo-Saxon and Norman England, <u>abbots</u> were <u>influential figures</u> — some of them were close to the king. As <u>major landholders</u>, abbots owed <u>service</u> to the king just like <u>other lords</u> (see p.30).

2) The <u>ordinary monks</u> helped <u>poorer people</u> in the <u>local area</u>. They gave <u>food</u> to those who were <u>hungry</u> and <u>medical care</u> to those who were <u>ill</u>.

3) Monasteries played an important role in <u>education</u> (see p.58). They also contributed to <u>culture</u> with works of <u>art</u> and <u>literature</u>, as well as <u>music</u>.

4) Some monasteries were <u>sites of pilgrimage</u> (holy places that worshippers visited). These sites were often associated with <u>saints</u> and owned <u>relics</u>. Monks provided <u>accommodation</u> for pilgrims visiting their monasteries.

5) Many of the saints that people worshipped stayed the same <u>before</u> and <u>after 1066</u>. The Normans had <u>different traditions</u>, but they preserved <u>existing saints</u> in an attempt to keep the Anglo-Saxons <u>satisfied</u>.

> <u>Relics</u> were items that were believed to have belonged to a <u>saint</u>, like <u>personal possessions</u> or even <u>body parts</u>. Monasteries could <u>earn money</u> by charging pilgrims to see these relics.

Life in a Norman Monastery

Try these activities to make sure you're confident about the different aspects of monasteries and monastic life.

Knowledge and Understanding

1) Why did monks live separately from other people?

2) Describe each of the following aspects of monastic life for a Benedictine monk:

a) Services   b) Work   c) Diet

3) Explain how monks contributed to wider society.

Thinking Historically

1) Copy and complete the table below, explaining whether there was change or continuity in each aspect of monasteries between Anglo-Saxon England and Norman England.

Aspect of monasteries	Change or continuity?	Explanation for choice
a) Buildings		
b) Services		
c) Saints		

Interpretation

This interpretation shows a cloister in a Norman monastery.

1) Explain whether you think each feature of the interpretation labelled below is convincing about what a Norman monastery was like.

a) Large windows

b) Stone pillars

c) Monks

d) A monk writing a book

© Look and Learn

EXAM TIP

All work and no pray made a monk a dull boy...

If you get an image as an interpretation in the exam, don't just describe what's in the image — you'll need to use your knowledge to explain whether it accurately reflects Norman England.

The Norman Church and Monasticism

Education and Literacy

Monks were some of the only people who could read and write, making them pretty useful to everyone else.

Most Written Texts came from Monasteries

1) All monks had to be able to read, and some of them were also able to write. Monks who could write often worked as scribes.

2) Scribes spent a lot of time making copies of existing texts, like the Bible. They also wrote new texts, like the Anglo-Saxon Chronicle.

3) Monks produced the books themselves, preparing all the materials they needed such as ink and parchment to write on. They also illustrated many of their books with bright colours or even decorated them with gold.

> The Anglo-Saxon Chronicle is a collection of historical accounts written by monks in several English monasteries, started in the 9th century. Monks continued adding to it until the 12th century, so parts of it were written after the Norman Conquest. It's one of the most important sources for modern historians studying Anglo-Saxon and Norman England.

Monks Taught People how to Read and Write

1) In Anglo-Saxon England, most people had little or no education. This didn't change under the Normans. Only wealthy families could afford to educate their children, and the small number of people who were educated were mostly taught by monks in monastic schools.

2) Many of the monks' pupils were boys who were sent to monasteries at a young age and brought up to become monks themselves. Other boys who were educated might become government officials.

3) The pupils in monastic schools learned to read and write, and were also taught Latin. They were expected to learn all the services (see p.56), as well as developing other useful skills such as discipline and obedience.

4) A small number of girls also received an education. They were mostly girls from wealthy families who were educated by nuns.

> Monasteries weren't the only places where people could receive an education — for example, some boys were taught at home by a private tutor. There were also secular schools, but these weren't as common.

The Conquest changed the Language used in England

1) Before 1066, Old English was the vernacular in England — it was the dominant spoken language in the country. However, the Anglo-Saxons wrote government documents and religious texts in the vernacular too. This was unusual in the rest of Western Europe, but it had been widespread in England since the 9th century.

2) In contrast, the Normans spoke Old French and used Latin in written documents.

> The vernacular is the language used by ordinary people in a particular area.

Spoken Language

After the Norman Conquest in 1066, Old English was still spoken by the majority of the population. However, the Norman settlers continued speaking Old French. This changed Old English significantly, because the Normans introduced a large number of French loanwords (words that are brought from one language into another) into English.

Written Language

After 1066, the main language for government documents and religious writing changed from Old English to Latin. At first, royal documents were issued in English to make sure they were understood. William then started to introduce Latin alongside English in bilingual documents. After 1070, these government documents were issued almost exclusively in Latin.

3) Although Latin became the dominant written language under the Normans, English monks continued to produce some written works in the vernacular — the Anglo-Saxon Chronicle (see above) was written in Old English even though parts of it were written after the conquest.

The Norman Church and Monasticism

Education and Literacy

These activities will help you get to grips with what education and language were like in Norman England.

Knowledge and Understanding

1) Using the key words below, describe how monks created books in Norman monasteries.

scribes   copies   new texts   materials   illustrated

2) Explain what is meant by the term 'vernacular'.

Interpretation

This image gives an interpretation of education in Norman England. It shows a boy and his teacher.

1) Explain whether you think the interpretation is convincing about each aspect of education in the boxes below.

a) Who provided education in Norman England

b) Who was given an education in Norman England

c) What pupils were taught in Norman England

Thinking Historically

1) Copy and complete the diagram below. State how spoken and written language changed after the Norman Conquest and explain why each type of language changed.

| Spoken Language | → | a) Change: | → | b) Explanation: |
| Written Language | → | c) Change: | → | d) Explanation: |

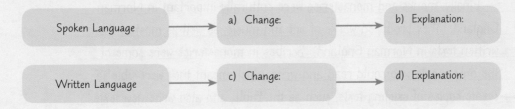

Monks put pupils on the write lines...

Interpretations can either be images or written texts. Although you'll only see one interpretation on the Normans in the exam, you should make sure you're comfortable analysing both types.

EXAM TIP

Worked Exam-Style Question

One question in the exam will ask you to explain why a particular event, issue or development was important in Norman England. The sample answer below will show you how to tackle this type of question.

How were monks and monasteries important in Norman England? Explain your answer. [8 marks]

The first sentence in each paragraph addresses the question.

Monks and monasteries had political importance in Norman England, because abbots helped to run the country. As well as being the chief monks in England's monasteries, abbots were among the king's tenants-in-chief, meaning they were responsible for governing large areas of land. They were also expected to provide the king with knights and to share a portion of the income from their land with him. Abbots were therefore an important part of William's government and provided services to help him maintain control of England. To ensure abbots were loyal to him, William replaced Anglo-Saxon abbots with Norman supporters as part of his policy of 'Normanisation'. This ensured he could rely on abbots to support his rule and carry out their important political duties.

The answer links the importance of monks and monasteries to the wider historical context of Norman England.

The answer covers different reasons why monks and monasteries were important in Norman England.

Monks and monasteries were also socially important because they provided services that were needed in Norman society. Monks helped poorer people in the local area by giving them food and medical care. Some monasteries were also sites of pilgrimage that were visited by worshippers, and monks would often provide accommodation for these visitors. These examples show how monks and monasteries contributed to important aspects of everyday life, such as health and worship. Another important social role that monks performed was educating people. Most wealthy families who could afford to educate their children sent them to monastic schools, where they were taught by monks. Pupils were taught reading, writing and Latin, and these skills prepared them for jobs that required them to be literate, such as a government official. Monks were therefore important in Norman England because they controlled what pupils learnt and had influence over people who would grow up to have important roles in Norman government and society.

The explanation links the point back to the question.

Finally, monks and monasteries were culturally important in Norman England. They produced works of art and music, as well as most of the written texts in Norman England. Scribes in monasteries were some of the only people who could read and write, which meant they were able to create copies of existing texts, such as the Bible, and also write new texts, including the Anglo-Saxon Chronicle. As scribes decided which texts were copied and produced, they had an important role in shaping literature and culture in Norman England.

Using specific facts and details shows a good understanding of the period.

The Norman Church and Monasticism

Exam-Style Questions

Try these exam-style questions to practise what you've learned about the Church in Norman England.

Interpretation 1

> For much of his reign, William I's relationship with the papacy was not a comfortable one. The power struggle between the king and the Pope raged throughout the 1070s and 1080s. However, on occasion it seemed that William had the upper hand, cleverly taking advantage of the papacy's weakness in order to make compromises that were to his benefit. William was not alone in his disputes with the papacy — Pope Gregory VII came into conflict with the rulers of many European countries during this time.

Exam-Style Questions

1) To what extent is Interpretation 1 convincing about William I's relationship with the papacy? Use Interpretation 1 and your own knowledge to explain your answer.   [8 marks]

2) How was the appointment of Archbishop Lanfranc important for Norman England? Explain your answer.   [8 marks]

3) Give an account of the ways that monasticism changed after the Norman Conquest.   [8 marks]

Answers

Marking the Activities

We've included sample answers for all the activities. When you're marking your work, remember that our answers are just a <u>guide</u> — some of the activities ask you to give your own <u>opinion</u>, so there is <u>no 'correct answer'</u>.

Marking the Exam-Style Questions

For each exam-style question, we've covered some <u>key points</u> that your answer could include. Our answers are just <u>examples</u> though — answers very different to ours could also get top marks.

Most exam questions in history are <u>level marked</u>. This means the examiner puts your answer into one of several <u>levels</u>. Then they award <u>marks</u> based on how well your answer matches the description for that level.

To reach a higher level, you'll need to give a '<u>more sophisticated</u>' answer. Exactly what 'sophisticated' means will depend on the type of question, but, generally speaking, a more sophisticated answer could include <u>more detail</u>, <u>more background knowledge</u> or make a <u>more complex judgement</u>.

Start by choosing which <u>level</u> your answer falls into. A good way to do this is to start at 'Level 1' and <u>go up to the next level</u> each time your answer meets <u>all</u> the conditions of a level. Next, choose a mark. The mark you choose will depend on whether you think you've met <u>all</u> of, <u>most</u> of, or <u>some</u> of the conditions in that level.

Level Descriptions:

Interpretation questions:

Level 1 1-2 marks	There is a basic analysis of one aspect of the interpretation. The answer shows limited knowledge and understanding of the period.
Level 2 3-4 marks	The answer gives a simple analysis of one aspect of the interpretation. It demonstrates some knowledge and understanding of the period.
Level 3 5-6 marks	The answer gives a developed analysis of more than one aspect of the interpretation. A good level of knowledge and understanding of the period is shown.
Level 4 7-8 marks	The answer gives a complex analysis of more than one aspect of the interpretation. Knowledge and understanding of the period is precise and detailed.

Importance questions:

Level 1 1-2 marks	The answer considers one aspect of the topic in the question, giving a basic explanation of its importance. The answer shows limited relevant knowledge and understanding of the period.
Level 2 3-4 marks	The answer considers one aspect of the topic in the question, giving a simple explanation of its importance. The answer shows some relevant knowledge and understanding of the period.
Level 3 5-6 marks	The answer considers two or more aspects of the topic in the question, giving a developed explanation of their importance. The answer shows a good level of relevant knowledge and understanding of the period.
Level 4 7-8 marks	The answer considers two or more aspects of the topic in the question, giving a detailed explanation of their importance within the wider historical context of Norman England. The answer shows an excellent level of relevant knowledge and understanding of the period.

Narrative account questions:

Level 1 1-2 marks	There is a basic analysis of the topic in the question. The answer gives a basic account that shows limited relevant knowledge and understanding of the period.
Level 2 3-4 marks	There is a simple analysis of the topic in the question. The answer gives an ordered account that shows some relevant knowledge and understanding of the period.
Level 3 5-6 marks	There is a developed analysis of the topic in the question. The answer gives a clear and well-structured account that shows a good level of relevant knowledge and understanding of the period.
Level 4 7-8 marks	There is a complex analysis of the topic in the question. The answer gives a logical and well-structured account that shows an excellent level of precise and detailed knowledge and understanding of the period.

Answers

The Normans: Conquest and Control

Page 9 — King Edward and the Godwins
Knowledge and Understanding

1 a) The King of England from 1042 to 1066.
   b) The last Scandinavian King of England before Edward took the throne.
   c) The Earl of Wessex from 1018, making him one of the most powerful men in England.
   d) Godwin's son. He was Earl of East Anglia and then became Earl of Wessex when his father died.
   e) Godwin's daughter. She was King Edward's wife and the Queen of England.
   f) Godwin's sons. They were also earls in England.

2 • 978 — Edward's father, Aethelred II, becomes King of England.
   • 1013 — Scandinavians invade England and take control of the country. Edward flees to Normandy after the invasion.
   • 1018 — Godwin becomes Earl of Wessex, giving him control of the oldest and richest earldom in England.
   • 1042 — Harthacnut dies. Edward returns to England and becomes king. Godwin supports Edward's claim to the throne.
   • 1051 — Godwin rebels against the king. He is sent into exile by Edward.
   • 1052 — Godwin returns to England with an army. Edward doesn't want to fight Godwin, so he makes Godwin Earl of Wessex again.
   • 1053 — Godwin dies and his son Harold is made Earl of Wessex. This makes Harold the most powerful man in England except for King Edward.

3 • Edward quickly gained the support of the three most powerful earls in England — Godwin of Wessex, Siward of Northumbria and Leofric of Mercia.
   • Edward prepared to defend his throne from foreign threats. He maintained a fleet in order to defend against an invasion from King Magnus of Norway.
   • Edward gave important positions in the royal household and the Church to his Norman followers.

4 The Godwins held a lot of land and controlled large areas of the kingdom. This helped them gain a lot of wealth, which they used to acquire a large number of followers and grant gifts to their allies. The Godwins' military strength also contributed to their power — for example, Godwin's military strength allowed him to regain his position as Earl of Wessex in 1052 after he was exiled.

Thinking Historically

1 a) Edward had a lot of power over the Godwins and asserted his authority over them. When Godwin rebelled unsuccessfully against Edward in 1051, Edward was able to send him into exile. This shows that Edward had the ability to take away the Godwins' power.
   b) The Godwins were a powerful family and Edward struggled to control them. When Godwin returned to England in 1052, Edward didn't want to fight Godwin's army so made him Earl of Wessex again. This led to the Godwins' return to power, suggesting that Edward's power over the Godwins was limited.
   c) Overall, Edward did not have a lot of power over the Godwins. While he was able to exile Godwin initially, he was not able to prevent Godwin's return to power as Earl of Wessex. This suggests that Edward did not have enough authority or military strength over the Godwins to remove them permanently as a powerful family in England.

2 Edward didn't have any children, so when he died there was no clear successor to the throne. This gave many people the opportunity to claim the throne. For example, there were claimants from Normandy because Edward had spent a lot of his life in Normandy and favoured his Norman supporters after he became King of England. There were also claimants from Scandinavia, because three of the Kings of England before Edward had been Scandinavians, meaning there were people from this region who felt they could claim the throne.

Page 11 — Claimants to the Throne in 1066
Knowledge and Understanding

1 a) Harold Godwinson was the most powerful nobleman in England. He was very ambitious and wanted to become king to secure his authority.
   b) William was the Duke of Normandy. He wanted to become king because it would make him more powerful and give him the same high status as the King of France.
   c) Harald Hardrada was the King of Norway. He wanted to take back the empire that had belonged to King Cnut, a former Scandinavian ruler of England.

2 Being related to the king was an important factor that could give someone a strong claim to the throne. Military strength was also an important factor as a claimant needed to be able to take control of the country.

3 Norman Sources:
   • Harold was sent to Normandy by Edward to name William as the heir to the English throne.
   • Harold swore an oath to support William's claim to the throne.
   English Sources:
   • Some sources say Harold went to Normandy to secure the release of his brother and nephew, who were hostages there.
   • Other sources suggest Harold was shipwrecked in northern France during a fishing trip.
   • The sources suggest that Harold swore an oath to William, but some say that William forced him to do it.

Thinking Historically

1 a) Strengths:
      • Edgar was related to King Edward.
      Weaknesses:
      • He was only a teenager.
      • He hadn't proven himself as a leader.
   b) Strengths:
      • Harold was the most powerful nobleman in England.
      • He was close to the royal family. His father, Godwin, had helped Edward become king, and his sister, Edith, was the queen.
      • Harold claimed Edward had asked him to be king on his deathbed.
      • Harold was an experienced military leader.
      Weaknesses:
      • He wasn't related to Edward.
      • He had supposedly made an oath to support William's claim to the throne.
   c) Strengths:
      • William was a powerful and successful military leader.
      • Some sources claim that Edward had promised William the throne, and Harold had sworn to support his claim.
      • He had a lot of experience as a ruler.
      • The Pope supported his claim, suggesting God was on his side.
      • He was related to Edward.

Weaknesses:
- There was uncertainty about whether Edward had promised him the throne.

d) Strengths:
- Harald was an experienced ruler.
- He was known for his military prowess.

Weaknesses:
- He claimed he was heir to England's Scandinavian kings, rather than to Edward.

2   You can choose any of the claimants, as long as you explain your answer. For example:
William had the strongest claim to the throne in 1066. He was related to Edward and was also a skilled military leader who had great success in stabilising Normandy in the past. This made him a more suitable leader than Edgar, who had no military experience. Although other claimants also had military experience, such as Harold and Hardrada, neither of them were related to Edward.

3   You can choose any of the claimants, as long as you explain your answer. For example:
Edgar Atheling had the weakest claim to the throne. Although he was related to Edward, he had no military experience or experience of ruling a kingdom. Other claimants who were related to Edward, such as William, had more experience than Edgar.

Page 13 — The Struggle for the Throne

Knowledge and Understanding

1 a) A part-time military force made up of ordinary people. They could be summoned away from their normal work when the king required men to fight. They only served for two months at a time.

   b) A professional, well-trained warrior.

2   • Mid-1066 — Harold and his army wait to defend the south coast of England against a Norman invasion.
   • Early September 1066 — Supplies start to run low and the fyrd need to return home to collect the harvest. Harold dismisses the fyrd and returns to London. Soon after, Harald Hardrada and Tostig invade north-eastern England.
   • 20th September 1066 — Earls Edwin and Morcar fight Hardrada at the Battle of Gate Fulford. The Anglo-Saxon forces are defeated.
   • 25th September 1066 — Harold defeats Hardrada at the Battle of Stamford Bridge. Hardrada and Tostig are killed, as is a large part of their army. The rest of the defeated army withdraws.
   • 28th September 1066 — The Normans land near Pevensey and begin pillaging Harold's lands.
   • 14th October 1066 — The Anglo-Saxon and Norman armies fight at the Battle of Hastings. Harold and his brothers, Gyrth and Leofwine, die in battle. The Anglo-Saxon army is defeated.

Thinking Historically

1 a) The Anglo-Saxons lost.
   • The Anglo-Saxon leaders Edwin and Morcar were inexperienced compared to Hardrada, who was an experienced military leader.
   • The Scandinavian army were more experienced fighters than the Anglo-Saxon army.

   b) The Anglo-Saxons won.
   • Harold's army consisted of professional fighters, the housecarls.
   • Hardrada didn't take his whole army to Stamford Bridge because he wasn't expecting a battle.

• Harold's fast march north meant he took Hardrada and the Scandinavian army by surprise — this gave him an advantage in the battle.

2 a) The Normans used the feigned flight tactic, pretending to run away from the Anglo-Saxons. This caused some of the Anglo-Saxons to chase the fleeing Normans, leaving their positions in the shield wall, which they had formed to defend against the Norman attack. This allowed the Norman army to break through the Anglo-Saxon defences, which contributed to the Normans' victory.

   b) Harold rushed into battle, so he didn't have time to gather all of his troops and his men didn't have enough time to recover from the long march or the Battle of Stamford Bridge. This meant his army was smaller than it could have been and in a weakened condition when he fought the Norman army.

   c) • The Normans landed in England when Harold's army was in the north and the south coast was undefended. This meant that there was no resistance waiting for the Normans when they arrived in England, which put them in a stronger position to fight at the Battle of Hastings.
   • When the Normans landed, the Anglo-Saxon army had just fought at the Battle of Stamford Bridge. This meant the Anglo-Saxons were tired from fighting and in a worse condition than the Norman troops.

Page 15 — Norman Military Tactics

Thinking Historically

1   Similarities:
   • Both armies had foot-soldiers.
   • Both armies included professional fighters — the Norman army was made up entirely of professional fighters and the Anglo-Saxons had the housecarls.

   Differences:
   • The Anglo-Saxon army was almost entirely made up of troops who fought on foot. The Norman army included cavalry, who fought on horseback.
   • The Norman army used archers, who could fight from a distance, whereas the Anglo-Saxon army didn't often use archers in battle.
   • The Anglo-Saxon army included the fyrd, who weren't as experienced or disciplined as the professional Norman army.
   • The Anglo-Saxon army usually created a shield wall, whereas the Normans used a wider variety of tactics, including feigned flight.

Knowledge and Understanding

1 a) These castles were built when William first invaded England. They gave him a strong base from which he could fight for the English throne.

   b) They were built on the south coast to protect England from an invasion by sea.

   c) They were built on the Welsh border to defend England against potential attacks from Wales.

   d) It was built after the Normans defeated a rebellion in Exeter in 1068.

2   The Anglo-Saxons didn't have much experience of fighting against enemies in castles, which made it harder for them to overcome the Normans' defences. Their fortifications were also less advanced than the Normans' castles, meaning the Anglo-Saxons struggled to defend against Norman attacks.

3
- Castles were used as strong defensive positions against Anglo-Saxon attacks.
- Castles were used to control strategically important places such as towns, major roads and rivers. This meant Normans across the country couldn't get cut off from each other and it also made it hard for Anglo-Saxon rebels to move around the country freely.
- A network of castles was built throughout England so soldiers could be stationed all over the country, allowing them to deal with local rebellions.
- Castles were used as bases to launch attacks on surrounding territory.

Page 17 — The Design of Norman Castles
Knowledge and Understanding
1 a) The motte was a cone-shaped mound of earth with a flat top, normally built next to a bailey but sometimes built inside it. Mottes ranged from 3m to 30m in height and were usually manmade.
  b) The bailey was an enclosed space surrounded by high walls. It was usually on one side of the motte and built on raised earthworks. The bailey contained most of the castle's living accommodation, such as housing, stables and a chapel.
  c) The keep, sometimes known as the tower, was a structure built at the top of the motte.
2 Wooden castles could be built quickly and without skilled labour. When the Normans first arrived in England, it was important for them to build castles quickly to help them establish control in England.
3 a) Richmond Castle was built next to a steep drop into the River Swale.
  b) Exeter Castle was just a fortified enclosure and didn't have a motte or a keep.
  c) Pevensey Castle was built inside a fortification that had existed before the conquest.

Thinking Historically
1 a) The ditch surrounded the motte and bailey and could be filled with water to create a moat, making it difficult for attackers to reach the motte and bailey. Ditches sometimes separated the motte and bailey, meaning the motte could be defended even if the bailey was captured.
  b) The raised earthworks were used as a base to build the motte and bailey on. This created a high bank, which made the castle easier to defend.
  c) The palisade was a fence of sharpened wooden stakes. Palisades were often built around the motte and the bailey to make it more difficult for attackers to climb over the wall and get inside.
  d) The bridge was the only way of crossing the ditch to reach the bailey. At the end of the bridge was a gatehouse where guards could be stationed. This made it difficult for attackers to enter the bailey and helped to protect the motte, which could only be reached by going through the bailey.

Page 19 — Resistance to Norman Rule, 1067-1069
Knowledge and Understanding
1 a) The Anglo-Saxons were supported by a French noble, Eustace II of Boulogne, in an unsuccessful attack on Dover Castle in Kent. It's possible that Eustace helped because he wanted to take control of Dover.
  b) Eadric the Wild, an Anglo-Saxon thegn, attacked Hereford Castle after his lands were seized by the Normans.
  c) The revolt in Exeter was probably caused by a rise in taxes. William promised to protect the town's inhabitants after they surrendered.

  d) At the same time as the Exeter revolt, Harold Godwinson's sons raided south-west England by sea.
  e) Edwin, Earl of Mercia, and Morcar, the former Earl of Northumbria, rebelled in Mercia. They were supported by the Welsh. William treated Edwin and Morcar leniently after the rebellion, granting them their lives and their freedom.
2 a) William hurries north and puts down the rebellion. He also builds a second castle at York and strengthens the Norman forces in Northumbria.
  b) The Danes help the remaining northern rebels take York, capturing both Norman castles there and taking control of Northumbria.
  c) William is able to scatter the Anglo-Saxon rebels, who no longer have the support of the Danes. He regains control of Northumbria.
3
- The Anglo-Saxon rebels in different places were motivated by local concerns, so they didn't form a national movement with common goals.
- There wasn't a single, strong leader who was backed by all the rebels.
- The rebels didn't coordinate their uprisings using a shared strategy.
- The rebels weren't supported by all Anglo-Saxons — many English nobles supported William and fought for him, while others didn't take sides.

Interpretation
1 a) This phrase is convincing because it suggests that there were many Anglo-Saxon rebellions. This reflects the fact that there were lots of Anglo-Saxon revolts all across the country between 1067 and 1069, including Eadric the Wild's rebellion in Hereford and Edwin and Morcar's in Mercia.
  b) This phrase is convincing because it shows that there were many factors that contributed to the failure of the Anglo-Saxon resistance. For example, the Anglo-Saxon rebels lacked a shared strategy and didn't have the backing of many English nobles.
  c) This phrase is convincing because it suggests that William had an important role in ending the Anglo-Saxon resistance. William personally went north to put down the northern revolt in 1069, which was a serious threat to his rule. During this revolt, William made an agreement with the Danes, who returned to their ships. This was key to ending the revolt as it left the Anglo-Saxon rebels unsupported, allowing William to scatter them.

Page 21 — The Harrying of the North
Knowledge and Understanding
1 The Harrying of the North was William's response to the 1069 rebellion, where he laid waste to large parts of northern England.
2 The northern revolt in 1069 had been a serious threat to William, and there were also other rebellions taking place all over the country. William's aim with the Harrying was to prevent future rebellions in the north by destroying the northern rebels' supplies and support. He also wanted to deter other rebellions by sending a message to the rest of the country about what to expect if they rebelled.

Interpretation
1 a) This feature is convincing because the Normans burnt down villages in the north of England as part of the Harrying of the North. This was intended to punish the Anglo-Saxons for revolting against the Normans.

Answers

b) This feature is convincing because it shows that the Normans used 'scorched earth' tactics during the Harrying of the North. The Normans deliberately destroyed food supplies and livestock such as cows, which led to a famine in the north of England. According to one source, there was so little food that some Anglo-Saxons resorted to eating dogs, cats and horses to survive.

2 The interpretation doesn't give a complete view of how William treated the Anglo-Saxons as it only presents his use of brutality against them. After some revolts, such as the northern revolt in 1069, William treated the Anglo-Saxons harshly. However, after other rebellions, William treated Anglo-Saxons who had rebelled against him more leniently. For example, he granted Edwin and Morcar their lives and freedom after their rebellion in Mercia in 1068.

Thinking Historically

1
- Villages were burned and destroyed.
- People starved because the Normans destroyed food and livestock.
- Many northerners became refugees and fled to other parts of England or to Scotland.
- Many people who stayed in the north after the Harrying faced disease.
- Northerners joined other rebellions, such as the one led by Hereward the Wake in East Anglia.
- The economy of the north was damaged.

2 You can answer either way, as long as you explain your answer. For example:
- William could have maintained control of England without the Harrying of the North. William had successfully put down every Anglo-Saxon rebellion against him, showing he was capable of maintaining control of England without resorting to such cruel tactics. For example, he put down the rebellions in 1067 and 1068 by building castles and using his military strength. This shows that there were other methods William could have used to maintain control of England instead of the Harrying of the North.
- William could not have maintained control of England without the Harrying of the North. He had tried peaceful methods of keeping Anglo-Saxons on his side such as treating Anglo-Saxon rebels like Morcar and the inhabitants of Exeter leniently. Despite this, there were still many Anglo-Saxon rebellions. Therefore, William needed to find a more effective way of maintaining control and deterring future rebellions. The Harrying achieved this because it sent a powerful message to the rest of the country about what to expect if they rebelled. Another reason why William could not have maintained control without the Harrying is that the 1069 revolt posed a serious threat to him because the rebels were a large force made up of the Anglo-Saxons, the Scottish and the Danes. While dealing with this, William was also facing other rebellions elsewhere in the country. This serious threat meant William had little choice but to carry out the Harrying in order to maintain control of the country by forcing the northern rebels to submit.

Page 23 — Resistance to Norman Rule, 1070-1075

Knowledge and Understanding
1 a) William pays the Danes to abandon Hereward.
   b) Hereward and Morcar take control of the Isle of Ely and try to hold it against William's army.
   c) Hereward survives the attack on Ely, but his whereabouts and actions after the rebellion in East Anglia are unknown.

2 They felt they had less power and influence than their fathers had done and they resented William for restricting their power.

3 a) Roger made an alliance with Ralph de Gael, and then joined forces with Earl Waltheof. During the revolt, he barely made it out of Hereford before being captured.
   b) Ralph made an alliance with Roger de Breteuil and married Emma, Roger's sister. He also made an alliance with Earl Waltheof. During the revolt, he escaped the siege of Norwich Castle and went to Denmark for reinforcements.
   c) Emma was left in control of Norwich Castle during its long siege, but eventually surrendered to the Norman forces.
   d) Waltheof joined forces with Ralph de Gael and Roger de Breteuil. He later betrayed the rebels by confessing the plans of the revolt to King William.
   e) Lanfranc was acting as regent in England at the time of the revolt. After William told him about Waltheof's confession, he reacted swiftly, sending troops to Roger and Ralph's earldoms and ending the revolt.
   f) The Danes came to England to support the revolt after Ralph de Gael asked for their assistance, but arrived too late to provide support to the rebels.

4 Earl Waltheof was treated more harshly than Roger and Ralph. Waltheof was the only one who was executed for his part in the rebellion. Roger was imprisoned for life and Ralph gave up his lands and went into exile.

Thinking Historically
1 Here are some points your answer may include:
- The only Anglo-Saxon earl involved in the revolt was beheaded, while the foreign earls were treated more leniently. This may have suggested that there were more serious consequences for Anglo-Saxons who rebelled, making them more reluctant to revolt.
- There had been many Anglo-Saxon rebellions between 1067 and 1075, but none of them had succeeded in overthrowing Norman rule. The Anglo-Saxons might have been so demoralised by these repeated failures that they no longer had the will to rebel.
- This was the first major revolt to involve foreign earls, who were far more powerful than the Anglo-Saxons. However, even with their power the revolt was unsuccessful. This may have suggested that William was too powerful to resist and made the Anglo-Saxons feel there was no way they could overthrow the Normans.

2 a) Roger de Breteuil was from Normandy and Ralph de Gael was from Brittany. As they weren't Anglo-Saxons, Roger and Ralph would have been expected to be loyal to William. However, their revolt showed that some of William's own supporters were dissatisfied with how he was running the kingdom. The Norman nobility were key to William's control of the country, making their revolt a serious threat to William's rule.
   b) The earls' lands gave them a lot of wealth and power. Together, the earls held lands across England — Waltheof held lands in Northumbria, Roger in Hereford and Ralph in East Anglia. Their control over large areas of the country made them more of a threat to William.
   c) William being in Normandy meant he couldn't personally help to put the revolt down and had to rely on his regent, Lanfranc, to end the threat to his rule.

Page 25 — William I and William II
Knowledge and Understanding
1 Before the rebellions, William tried to work with the Anglo-Saxon nobles. After the rebellions between 1068 and 1071, he didn't care about keeping the Anglo-Saxons happy.

2   Normanisation was the process of making England 'more Norman' by replacing Anglo-Saxons with Normans in areas such as government and the Church. The redistribution of land is another example of Normanisation.

3
- Robert Curthose, William's eldest son, became Duke of Normandy.
- William Rufus, William's second son, became King of England.
- Henry, William's youngest son, was given £5000.

4
- 9th September 1087 — While at war with the King of France, William dies from a serious injury.
- 26th September 1087 — William II is crowned King of England by Lanfranc.
- 1088 — Odo of Bayeux leads a rebellion against William II, believing that Robert Curthose should be King of England. However, the rebellion fails and Odo is sent into exile by William II.
- 1096 — Robert gives Normandy to William II, meaning William controls both Normandy and England.

5   Odo was unable to get enough support for the rebellion because most of the lords remained loyal to William II. Robert and his reinforcements remained in Normandy, leaving Odo unsupported.

Thinking Historically

1 a) Normanisation involved making England 'more Norman'. For example, William took away lands belonging to the Anglo-Saxons and gave them to loyal Normans instead. This gave William's followers more power while reducing the power of the Anglo-Saxons. William also replaced Anglo-Saxons in the Church and government with Norman supporters, meaning William had loyal followers in influential roles. Normanisation helped William maintain control because it increased Norman influence in England and reduced Anglo-Saxon influence.

   b) The Normans were encouraged to marry the widows and daughters of Anglo-Saxons who had previously owned land. This helped to make Norman control of the land seem more legitimate. Having control over English lands meant William's supporters had more power, which helped him maintain control over the country.

   c) Castles were used by lords to govern the surrounding areas. They became centres of local government where taxes were collected and law and order was enforced. This use of castles helped William maintain control by helping to ensure that the kingdom was governed effectively.

   d) William used regents to govern England when he was in Normandy. Regents had the same authority as the king, ensuring that the country was ruled effectively during William's absences.

Page 27 — Exam-Style Questions

1   This question is level marked. You should look at the level descriptions on page 62 to help you mark your answer. Here are some points your answer may include:
- The interpretation is convincing about the challenges William Rufus faced because it explains that his claim to the throne was 'controversial'. The Normans followed a system of primogeniture, which meant that the eldest son inherited a lord's lands when the lord died. As Robert Curthose was William I's eldest son and William Rufus was younger, the custom of primogeniture may have led people to expect that Robert would become King of England. This meant William Rufus had to overcome these expectations in order to become king.

- The interpretation is convincing because it shows that William Rufus had to act quickly to secure his claim to the throne as a result of the challenges he faced. The interpretation states that he 'moved quickly' to claim England. William Rufus sailed for England a couple of days before his father's death and quickly gained the support of Lanfranc, who crowned him as King of England on 26th September 1087.

- The reference to 'discontent' after William II became king makes the interpretation convincing. Many lords held land in England and Normandy, so this meant they had to serve both William and Robert Curthose, who was Duke of Normandy. This created problems for the lords because it meant they had to divide their loyalties between two competing rulers. As a result, many lords felt their lives would be easier if England and Normandy were united under one ruler.

- The interpretation is convincing because it shows the 'tension' William II faced among his nobles. This refers to the rebellion against William II in 1088, when Odo of Bayeux and a number of other lords attempted to remove him from the throne. However, the interpretation is not entirely convincing because it does not mention that some lords were happy with William II as king. William crushed Odo's rebellion with the help of many lords who were loyal to him.

- The interpretation convincingly presents the conflict between William and his brother Robert. Although Robert became Duke of Normandy after his father's death, he believed England should also belong to him and that William II had wrongfully seized the throne. Robert and William continued to fight each other until 1096, when Robert gave Normandy to William, which shows the 'tension' between the two brothers.

2   This question is level marked. You should look at the level descriptions on page 62 to help you mark your answer. Here are some points your answer may include:
- Castles were important because they helped the Normans conquer England in 1066. When the Normans landed at Pevensey, they built a castle there and also built one at Hastings before the battle. This gave the Normans a strong base from which to fight against the Anglo-Saxons, contributing to their victory at the Battle of Hastings and creating the foundation for the beginning of Norman England.

- The castles built after the Battle of Hastings were important because they helped the Normans defend England against foreign threats. The Normans built castles along the south coast in places such as Dover, Arundel and Corfe to protect England from an invasion by sea. They also built castles along the Welsh border in places such as Chester and Hereford to stop an invasion from Wales. This helped the Normans to stop foreign forces that wanted to oppose Norman rule or support Anglo-Saxon rebels.

- Castles were important because they gave the Normans a military advantage over the Anglo-Saxons. The Anglo-Saxons didn't have a lot of experience of warfare involving castles. Their fortifications used simple features such as ditches, earth banks and fences, but were significantly less advanced than the motte and bailey castles used by the Normans. This meant the Anglo-Saxons struggled to attack Norman fortifications and were unable to effectively defend the land that they did hold. This helped the Normans to establish and maintain control over England after 1066.

Answers

- Castles helped the Normans to secure strategically important locations, which was important for maintaining control of England. The Normans used castles to control towns, major roads and rivers so that Norman forces across the country wouldn't get cut off from each other. This also made it difficult for Anglo-Saxon rebels to move around the country freely, which limited the effectiveness of their rebellions against the Normans.
- Castles were important in the establishment of Norman England because they allowed the Normans to put down Anglo-Saxon rebellions quickly. William I built a network of castles throughout England. This meant he could station Norman soldiers all over the country who could be called upon to deal with local rebellions. This was particularly important in the first years after the conquest, when the Normans faced Anglo-Saxon rebellions across the country. For example, in 1069, the Normans were able to deal with rebellions in Shrewsbury, the west country and Mercia using local forces that were stationed in castles.
- Castles were important in helping William govern the country effectively. The lords in charge of castles were responsible for governing the surrounding area. This meant castles became centres of local government where taxes were collected and law and order was enforced. Castles therefore helped local government to operate effectively, which was important in helping William maintain control of the country.

3   This question is level marked. You should look at the level descriptions on page 62 to help you mark your answer. Here are some points your answer may include:

- At first, William treated rebels who surrendered to him leniently. For example, after Edwin and Morcar rebelled in Mercia in 1068, William granted them their lives and freedom. Similarly, after the rebellion in Exeter, William promised to protect the town's inhabitants. William was lenient towards rebels early in his reign because, before 1070, his policy was to try and work with the Anglo-Saxon nobles and keep them on his side.
- After William's lenient approach failed to stop Anglo-Saxon rebellions, his response became harsher. In response to the northern rebellion in 1069, he ordered the Harrying of the North. The Normans burned down villages, slaughtered their inhabitants and used 'scorched earth' tactics to destroy food supplies and devastate large areas of northern England. William's response was harsher than in previous rebellions because the northern rebellion posed a serious threat to his rule. The rebellion involved foreign rulers such as King Malcolm III of Scotland and King Swein II of Denmark, and other rebellions were taking place across the country at the same time. William therefore responded harshly to the northern rebellion to force the northern rebels to submit and to send a powerful message to the rest of the country about what to expect if they rebelled.
- William's response to individual rebels became less lenient after 1070. After Morcar joined Hereward the Wake's rebellion in 1071, William imprisoned Morcar. William also executed Earl Waltheof for his role in the Revolt of the Earls, even though Waltheof confessed the plan to revolt to William, which allowed the revolt to be crushed quickly. William was less lenient than earlier in his reign because he no longer felt he had to satisfy the Anglo-Saxons.

- By 1075, William had less personal involvement in ending major rebellions. During the northern revolt in 1069, William played an active part in putting down the rebellion, coming to an agreement with the Danes, helping to scatter the Anglo-Saxon rebels and leading the Harrying of the North. However, during the Revolt of the Earls in 1075, William didn't even return from Normandy. Instead, when he received a warning from Earl Waltheof of Northumbria that the rebellion was going to happen, he passed on the information to his regent Lanfranc and left him to deal with the rebels. This change was possible because, by 1075, William had established his authority in England so firmly that he was comfortable spending time away from the country while his regents ruled in his absence.

Life Under the Normans
Page 29 — Norman Society
Knowledge and Understanding

1   The king in Anglo-Saxon England was responsible for protecting the country from invaders. He was also the head of the government and oversaw the running of the country. The king owned the largest amount of land, making him the richest and most powerful person in the kingdom. However, he still required the support of the upper nobility and lower nobility in order to rule.

2 a) Norman — They held land directly from the king. They included archbishops, bishops, abbots, earls and barons.
  b) Both — In Anglo-Saxon society, earls were the most powerful noblemen. They were given large areas of land by the king and were expected to make sure their earldoms were well governed. In Norman society, earls were some of the king's tenants-in-chief.
  c) Anglo-Saxon — Thegns were members of the lower nobility. They received land from their lord. They helped to govern the local area and provided military service.
  d) Norman — Knights were similar to thegns in Anglo-Saxon society, although the service they provided to their lord was almost always military. They were given land by their lord.

3 a) A person who had dependents relying on them for land and protection.
  b) Giving support to a person or an organisation. One type of patronage in Norman England was when a person gave land to someone and became their lord. Other types of patronage included the king giving his followers power and influence and nobles giving money and protection to the Church.
  c) The new social structure introduced to England by William I. Under the feudal system, the king had control and ownership of all the land in the kingdom.

Thinking Historically

1 a) Change — In Anglo-Saxon England, the king allowed his earls to own large areas of land. In Norman England, the king owned all of the land and his tenants-in-chief only held their land with his permission.
  b) Continuity — The role of a peasant didn't change much. They still farmed land for their lord as they had done in Anglo-Saxon England.
  c) Change — The number of slaves decreased after the conquest.

Answers

2   Under the Norman feudal system, the king owned all
     of the land, meaning he was very powerful. Norman
     tenants-in-chief held land with the king's permission, but as
     the king owned all the land he was able to take it away if
     he wanted to. This meant tenants-in-chief relied on the king
     for their power, which gave the king a lot of power over
     them. Therefore, the feudal system gave William a network
     of loyal supporters who could provide him with military
     service, and this helped him to secure the conquest.

Page 31 — Lordship and Landholding
Interpretation
1 a) The interpretation is convincing because it explains that
        vassals owed their lords 'financial and military support'.
        Tenants-in-chief would provide knights and give part of
        their income to the king, while knights would pay taxes
        and provide military service to their lord, such as protecting
        a castle, fighting in wars or protecting their lord while
        travelling. In return for their loyalty and service, vassals
        were given land by their lord.
   b) The interpretation is convincing because it says that
        peasants owed 'service and loyalty' to their lord. Although
        peasants didn't 'bend the knee' and do homage to their
        lord, they were still expected to be loyal to him and to give
        labour service on his land. In return, their lord would give
        them protection and the right to farm a patch of land for
        themselves.
   c) The interpretation is convincing because it claims that
        loyalty was at the 'centre' of the feudal system. The feudal
        system was designed to reward loyal service, as vassals
        swore an oath of loyalty to their lords and were given land
        in return. If a vassal broke this agreement, they might be
        forced to forfeit their land, which shows the importance of
        loyalty in the feudal system.

Knowledge and Understanding
1   The lands held by William's 'inner circle' were smaller than
     the earldoms that had belonged to earls in Anglo-Saxon
     England.
2   In Anglo-Saxon England, a landholder would divide his
     land equally between children when he died. However,
     the Normans used a different system of inheritance called
     primogeniture, which meant land was inherited by a
     landholder's eldest son. If a landholder died childless, the
     land returned to his lord.

Thinking Historically
1   The rebellions showed that William's policy of trying to
     work with the Anglo-Saxons wasn't working and they would
     continue to be a threat if he left them in power. Replacing
     the Anglo-Saxon nobles with Normans reduced this threat
     by reducing the Anglo-Saxons' power and making it harder
     for them to rebel.
2   William made estates smaller and more compact. This
     helped him to maintain control over England because it
     meant the estates were easier to defend against military
     threats. Making estates smaller also helped William
     maintain control because it reduced the power of noble
     families and ensured they didn't have enough strength to
     threaten him as king.
3 a) Primogeniture meant that the landholder's eldest son had
        to pay a tax to the lord to inherit the land. This helped the
        king and other lords to make money.
   b) Primogeniture helped to limit landholding to fewer people,
        which meant fewer people had power than in Anglo-Saxon
        England. It also stopped family estates becoming small and
        fragmented.

Page 33 — Norman Government
Knowledge and Understanding
1   Tenants-in-chief oversaw the government in their own
     lands, which covered relatively large areas of the country.
     The lands controlled by tenants-in-chief were divided
     into shires. These shires were governed by sheriffs. The
     shires were divided into smaller areas called hundreds,
     which were made up of multiple villages. Hundreds were
     controlled by sheriffs and their deputies.
2   By giving more power to sheriffs, William reduced the
     authority of earls and reduced their influence over how their
     lands were managed. This damaged William's relationship
     with his earls because some earls resented these changes.
     Some historians believe this resentment contributed to the
     Revolt of the Earls in 1075.
3   The royal demesne was the land that the king kept for
     himself. This made up around one quarter of all the land in
     England.
4   He didn't want them to become powerful enough to rebel
     against him.
5   In a centralised government, power is focused around one
     figure, e.g. in Norman England power was focused around
     the king.
6 a) The Curia Regis was the king's council. It was made up of
        the king's tenants-in-chief, who advised him and helped
        him govern the kingdom. It was similar to the Witan in
        Anglo-Saxon England.
   b) The chancery was responsible for producing documents,
        such as writs, that were needed to help William govern the
        country. It moved around the country with the king. The
        chancery hadn't existed in Normandy, so the idea might
        have come from the Anglo-Saxons.
   c) The treasury was responsible for managing royal income
        and also physically stored the king's own wealth.

Thinking Historically
1   Change:
     • Sheriffs were given more power.
     • They were able to perform their duties with less
       interference from earls.
     • Sheriffs became responsible for the royal demesne.
     • Sheriffs were wealthier and held more land than they had
       in Anglo-Saxon England.
     Continuity:
     • They supervised the collection of fines and taxes at a
       local level.
     • They judged criminal cases at local courts.
     • They organised and often led military forces.
     • Sheriffs were appointed by the king.
2 a) William increased the use of writs. This allowed him to give
        instructions to local government and take a more direct role
        in running the whole of the kingdom.
   b) William filled the government with Normans rather
        than with Anglo-Saxons. This meant that the people in
        government were more likely to support William, reducing
        the risk of rebellion from within the government.

Page 35 — The Norman Legal System
Knowledge and Understanding
1 a) Forest law was a new law that set aside large areas of the
        country as royal forest for William to hunt in. Ordinary
        people weren't allowed to use the royal forest and were
        severely punished if they did.

Answers

b) The 'murdrum' fine was a new punishment introduced by the Normans. If a Norman was murdered and the killer wasn't caught, the whole village where the Norman was murdered would have to pay a large fine. The fine was introduced to prevent Norman settlers being attacked or killed by Anglo-Saxons.

2 a) • The king's court was where the most important legal cases were heard.
   • The king and his royal officials were in charge of the king's court.

b) • The shire courts tried criminal cases and dealt with cases involving land and property.
   • The shire courts were usually overseen by sheriffs.

c) • The hundred courts were used for less serious crimes, such as stealing livestock or failing to repay small debts.
   • The hundred courts were overseen by sheriffs or their deputies.

d) • The manor courts dealt with everyday problems in villages, such as peasants who weren't working properly.
   • Lords were in charge of manor courts.

e) • Honourial courts resolved land disputes between a lord's vassals.
   • Lords were in charge of honourial courts.

3 a) There were different types of trial by ordeal. One of these involved throwing someone into water that had been blessed by a priest. If they floated, the water (and therefore God) was 'rejecting' them, meaning they were guilty. If they sank, the water was 'accepting' them, so they were innocent.

b) If someone was accused of a crime, they could challenge the accuser to a fight to the death. The Normans thought that if someone was innocent, then God would intervene and help them to win the fight.

Thinking Historically

1 a) William introduced some new laws, such as forest law and the 'murdrum' fine. However, he didn't change the laws that had existed during King Edward's reign.

b) William maintained the use of shire and hundred courts that had existed in Anglo-Saxon England. However, the Normans also introduced new honourial courts that lords could use to resolve land disputes between their vassals.

c) Some types of trials stayed the same, such as trial by ordeal. The Normans also introduced new ways of trying people, such as trial by combat.

2 • William didn't change many laws from before the conquest so he could create continuity with King Edward's reign. This was intended to show that he was Edward's legitimate successor.
   • The Normans kept much of the Anglo-Saxon legal system the same as it was well developed and worked well.
   • There were some aspects of the Anglo-Saxon legal system that hadn't existed in Normandy but that the Normans found useful, so they left them in place. This included the use of shire and hundred courts.
   • Some aspects of the Anglo-Saxon legal system already existed in Normandy, such as trial by ordeal, so the Normans continued to use them in England.

Page 37 — The Domesday Book
Knowledge and Understanding

1 The Domesday Book is a survey and valuation of all the land and resources in England, carried out in 1086. It contains records of the land held by the king, his tenants-in-chief and their vassals, as well as who held the land in 1066, how much the land was worth then and its value in 1086.

2 England was divided into shires and hundreds and governed locally, which made it possible to collect information for the Domesday Book. The Anglo-Saxon taxation records also provided information that was useful for the Domesday Book.

3 It gives detailed information from before and after the conquest. This helps historians study how England changed over time and lets them judge the impact that the conquest had on England.

4 a) Tenants-in-chief, alongside government officials in each shire, made lists of who owned the land and gave these to commissioners.

b) Commissioners compared lists of who owned the land with existing records about land ownership. They also asked juries about the ownership and value of land.

c) Juries were summoned from each hundred to special meetings of the shire courts to provide information about the ownership and value of land. They were made up of equal numbers of Anglo-Saxons and Normans to ensure that the information was accurate from before and after the conquest.

Interpretation

1 a) The interpretation is convincing as it mentions William's lords 'arguing about land', which refers to the disagreements between Normans and Anglo-Saxons over landownership between 1066 and 1086. It also refers to 'the threat of a foreign attack', which is convincing because the King of Denmark and his Norwegian allies threatened to invade England in 1085.

b) The interpretation is convincing because it claims that the Domesday Book was useful in helping with the 'defence of the country'. This reflects the fact that the book gave information about how many knights the king could summon to fight for him. This allowed the king to see what military resources were available to him.

c) The interpretation is convincing because it explains that the Domesday Book could be used to settle 'arguments over land'. The Domesday Book contained detailed information about who owned the land in England, and this helped to resolve legal disagreements over land by providing written evidence of who the land belonged to.

d) The interpretation is convincing because it explains that the Domesday Book gave the king 'greater control over his income'. The king could use the Domesday Book to make sure he was receiving the correct amount of money from his subjects. The Domesday Book provided a record of how much landowners' estates were worth, so the king could use it to make sure he was receiving all the taxes and other payments that landowners owed him. It also helped the king to figure out when someone had inherited land, allowing him to demand relief from them.

Page 39 — Life in Norman England
Knowledge and Understanding

1 a) Peasants would plough fields and plant seeds.
   b) Peasants would harvest the crops.

2 • Blacksmith
   • Carpenter

3 a) • Living conditions were unpleasant and unhygienic.
   • Peasants often lived in cramped conditions because they only had one room where the whole family lived.
   • Peasants' houses were very smoky because they had no windows and an open fire was used for warmth and cooking.

b) • Peasants' houses were usually made from wood or from wattle and daub (wooden strips that were stuck together with materials such as clay, soil and manure).
   • The floor was made of earth with a layer of straw on top of it.
4 Norman villages were in rural locations — they were surrounded by the fields where villagers grew crops.
5 • Church
   • Manor house
   • Mill

Thinking Historically

1 a) The conquest barely affected the population of villages in England. The peasants who lived in villages were still Anglo-Saxons. The only difference was that the lord who governed the village would probably be a Norman rather than an Anglo-Saxon.
   b) The conquest did not have much effect on the type of work done in villages. Peasants were still expected to farm their lord's land by ploughing fields and planting seeds.
   c) The conquest affected some buildings in English villages. The Normans rebuilt some buildings in stone, including many churches and manor houses. In some places, the Normans also built new buildings, such as a stone mill in the village of Wharram Percy.
2 a) • Meat was very expensive, so peasants couldn't afford to eat it. The rich ate a lot of meat because they could afford it.
   • The rich avoided eating fruit, vegetables and dairy because they were associated with the poor.
   b) • Peasants relied on a good harvest as they grew a lot of their food. They grew crops such as wheat, rye and barley, which they used to make bread. They might also grow fruit and vegetables.
   • If there was a bad harvest, peasants would go hungry or even starve.
   c) • Forest law limited the amount of land that peasants could hunt, fish or gather food in. This reduced their access to wild animals, fish and plants.

Page 41 — Life in Norman England

Knowledge and Understanding

1 • At first, buildings were destroyed and the local economy was badly damaged as a result of the conquest.
   • Many towns in Norman England were larger than in Anglo-Saxon England. As people moved to towns from rural areas, towns such as Nottingham grew in size.
   • New towns such as St Albans developed.
   • People from abroad started to settle in English towns.
   • Towns played a more important role in Norman England than in Anglo-Saxon England. After the conquest, towns became centres of trade and administration.
   • Towns had military and religious functions because castles, churches and cathedrals were built in towns.
   • There was an increased demand for goods and services from craftsmen because of the construction of new buildings.
   • For merchants in towns, there was an increase in trade with Normandy and the rest of France.
2 People who wanted to learn a trade would start out as an apprentice and work for a master craftsman to learn the skills of their trade. Eventually they would leave their master and earn money for themselves.
3 • Craftsmen and merchants traded goods and services on the high street, which was the main road through town.
   • People could buy and sell goods and services in the market square.

4 • Most people in villages worked the land, whereas people did a wide variety of jobs in towns, such as being butchers, bakers, tailors, shoemakers, carpenters and stone masons.
   • People in villages grew their own crops and kept their own animals for food. People who lived in towns were more likely to buy their food at markets.
   • Towns were crowded and busy compared to villages.

Interpretation

1 a) The phrase is convincing because it suggests that there was lots of construction work going on in towns in Norman England. The Normans built lots of castles, churches and cathedrals in towns after the conquest, which provided work for craftsmen like carpenters and stone masons.
   b) The phrase is convincing because it suggests that some towns changed significantly as a result of the conquest. In many towns, buildings were destroyed and the economy was damaged due to the events of the conquest and the rebellions that followed. However, towns began to recover in the years following the conquest as new buildings were constructed and the economy began to grow. All these changes mean that many towns were 'transformed' after the conquest.
   c) The phrase is convincing because it describes a building that has burnt down. This reflects the fact that fire was a serious risk in towns, because wooden houses were built close together on narrow streets, making it easy for fire to spread between them.
   d) The phrase is convincing because it shows that conditions in towns could be unhealthy. Rubbish and waste could build up quickly, and many people lived in cramped and unhygienic conditions. This meant that disease was common in towns, and this contributed to the low life expectancy for ordinary people in Norman England.

Page 43 — Exam-Style Questions

1 This question is level marked. You should look at the level descriptions on page 62 to help you mark your answer. Here are some points your answer may include:
   • The interpretation is convincing because it shows that most peasants were involved in farming. In the image, there is a peasant working in a field, a peasant feeding chickens and someone else herding livestock. This shows that farming was an important part of villagers' lives and reflects the fact that farming was vital to the economy of Norman England.
   • The interpretation is convincing because it shows that villagers sometimes learnt a trade. In the image there is a peasant working on a log of wood. This could suggest that he is a carpenter. Although the majority of peasants in villages farmed the land, some people did learn a trade because most villages required the skills of a blacksmith and a carpenter.
   • The interpretation convincingly reflects the type of food available to villagers in Norman England. The image shows someone feeding chickens, which reflects the fact that peasants often kept chickens to provide them with eggs. The image also shows someone working in the fields, showing how peasants would grow crops such as wheat, rye and barley, which they could use to make bread. There is also a forest in the background of the image which may refer to the fact that some peasants hunted and gathered food in forests, although this method of obtaining food was later limited by the introduction of forest law.

Answers

- The unpleasant living conditions of villages are presented convincingly in the interpretation. Peasant houses in villages often had only one room where a whole family lived, and the small houses in the image reflect these cramped conditions. The image also hints at the unhygienic living conditions in villages, as it depicts animals walking near the open doors of the houses.
- The location of villages in Norman England is presented convincingly in the interpretation. The image shows that the village is in a rural location where villagers are able to grow crops. This suggests that Norman villages were surrounded by fields which the peasants farmed.
- The interpretation convincingly reflects the impact the conquest had on buildings in villages. The image shows a castle and a church, both of which are made from stone. After the conquest, the Normans built lots of stone castles all across England to help them keep control of the country. They also built or rebuilt important buildings such as churches using stone. However, the Normans didn't replace all buildings. In the image, the peasant houses are made from wood, just as they would have been in Anglo-Saxon England.

2   This question is level marked. You should look at the level descriptions on page 62 to help you mark your answer. Here are some points your answer may include:
- Towns were important because they helped the Normans to maintain control of England. Towns were centres of administration, as the castles built in towns were used by lords to govern the local area. The castles in towns also housed soldiers who helped to deal with Anglo-Saxon rebellions, meaning that towns had important military functions. These functions of castles meant that towns were important because they helped the Normans to control the kingdom.
- Towns were important because they became centres of trade. Due to the conquest, England began to trade more with Normandy and the rest of France. This allowed merchants who worked in towns to export goods such as wool and import products such as wine and textiles. This trade in towns helped the economy to grow.
- Towns were important because they provided opportunities for a variety of jobs in Norman England. After the conquest, more people began to move to towns, which led to the growth of existing towns such as Nottingham and the development of new towns such as St Albans. This was important because it helped the economy of towns to recover and created more opportunities for work. For example, the construction of new churches and cathedrals in towns created a demand for carpenters and stone masons. People in towns could also become craftsmen in one of many trades, such as butcher, tailor or shoemaker. This was very different from the situation in villages, where there were fewer opportunities as most people had to farm the land.
- Towns were important because they contributed to the low life expectancy in Norman England. Many people in towns lived in wooden houses that were built on narrow streets, meaning fires could spread easily between them, and the houses were often cramped and unhygienic. Towns also had larger populations than villages, which resulted in rubbish and waste building up more quickly. These poor conditions meant that disease was common in towns, and this was a factor in Norman England's low life expectancy.

3   This question is level marked. You should look at the level descriptions on page 62 to help you mark your answer. Here are some points your answer may include:
- William I introduced a new law called forest law. This set aside large areas of land as royal forest for the king to hunt in. Before forest law was introduced, ordinary people were able to use the land to hunt, fish and gather food. After the introduction of forest law, however, ordinary people weren't allowed to use the royal forest and faced severe punishment if they did.
- William also introduced the 'murdrum' fine. This meant that if a Norman was murdered and the killer wasn't caught, the whole village where the Norman was murdered had to pay a large fine. This law was initially brought in to protect Norman settlers in the first years of the conquest. However, the law remained for the rest of William's reign because it was a useful source of income for the king.
- The Normans introduced trial by combat, which could be used to decide whether someone was guilty if a court couldn't reach a verdict. Trial by combat allowed someone who was accused of a crime to challenge the accuser to a fight to the death. The Normans believed that if someone was innocent, then God would intervene and help them to win the fight. The introduction of trial by combat after the conquest provided a different way to judge a person's guilt that hadn't existed in England before 1066.
- The Normans changed how legal disputes over land were dealt with by creating the Domesday Book in 1086. The Domesday Book contained accurate information about who land belonged to before 1066 and who owned it in 1086. The king could use the Domesday Book to end disagreements over landownership because it provided written evidence of who owned the land. Before the creation of the Domesday Book, disagreements over landownership were harder to resolve because Anglo-Saxon records weren't as comprehensive as the Domesday Book, and sometimes disagreements were resolved based only on people's word. This shows that the Normans introduced a more effective system for resolving legal disputes over landownership.
- The Normans made minor changes to the court system in England. One of the issues with the Anglo-Saxon legal system was that courts in different parts of the country often operated in different ways. The Normans reduced this inconsistency across the country. The Normans also introduced honourial courts to help lords deal with disputes in their own lands. These courts allowed a lord to resolve land disputes between their vassals.

The Norman Church and Monasticism

Page 45 — The Anglo-Saxon Church
Knowledge and Understanding
1   The Church was split up into sixteen dioceses. Each diocese was controlled by a bishop. Dioceses were starting to be divided into parishes by 1066.
2
- Ordinary people attended mass performed by a priest.
- The Church carried out ceremonies for ordinary people, such as baptisms and burials.
- Ordinary people confessed their sins and did penance before a priest.

Answers

3 a) Pluralism was the act of a churchman holding more than one religious office at the same time.

   b) Simony was the act of buying or selling religious offices and promotions.

   c) Nepotism was the act of giving positions in the Church to friends or family members.

   d) Clerical marriage was when churchmen had wives or mistresses, despite the fact they were meant to remain unmarried.

4 Stigand contributed to corruption by committing pluralism. He continued to hold the position of Bishop of Winchester after he became Archbishop of Canterbury.

Thinking Historically

1 Church:
   • It received gifts such as land and precious objects.
   • It received protection from violence and robbery.
   • It sometimes received the second-born sons of the nobility to train as priests, which helped the Church to grow.
   Nobility:
   • They sent their second-born sons to train as priests, which reduced competition for land within the nobility.
   • They had influence over the appointment of churchmen, meaning they could give important posts to their relatives and followers.
   • The Church said prayers for the nobility. The nobility believed prayers would help them have success on earth and get into heaven.

2 The king needed a good relationship with the Church because the Church was able to legitimise his claim to power. People believed a ruler needed God's support to be successful, and if the Church supported a king it was seen as a sign that God was on the king's side.

Page 47 — Norman Church Reform

Knowledge and Understanding

1 • Bishops — Each bishop was in charge of a diocese. They were appointed by the king and he chose skilled administrators who would stay loyal to him. Bishops were also lords, so they held land and provided knights for the king's armies.
   • Archdeacons — Each archdeacon was in charge of an archdeaconry. Archdeacons took responsibility for administration and discipline within their archdeaconry, which helped bishops run their dioceses. Archdeacons became more influential under the Normans due to the creation of archdeaconries.
   • Deans — Each dean was in charge of a deanery, which was made up of a group of parishes. Deans were responsible for making sure that the priests in their deanery were following religious law.
   • Priests — Each priest was in charge of a parish, which had its own church. Their responsibilities didn't change from Anglo-Saxon England, so they would still say mass regularly, perform key ceremonies such as baptisms and burials and get people to confess their sins and do penance.

Thinking Historically

1 The Church was a powerful institution in Norman England. It held large areas of land, played a role in the government and was able to influence ordinary people's opinions. Therefore, being in control of the Church gave the king a lot of power and influence which helped him to control the kingdom.

2 a) Change — The Normans reorganised certain dioceses by moving their headquarters from rural areas or small towns (e.g. Dorchester) to larger towns (e.g. Lincoln). They also divided dioceses into smaller areas called archdeaconries, which had not existed in the Anglo-Saxon Church.

   b) Change — William replaced the most powerful Anglo-Saxons in the English Church, such as archbishops and bishops, with his own supporters. For example, the Anglo-Saxon Archbishop of Canterbury, Stigand, was replaced with a supporter of William's called Lanfranc. By 1087, there was only one bishop in England who was Anglo-Saxon.

   c) Continuity — Churchmen at lower levels weren't replaced in the way that churchmen like archbishops and bishops were. After the conquest, there were still a lot of Anglo-Saxon monks and the majority of parish priests were Anglo-Saxon.

   d) Change — In Anglo-Saxon England, churchmen were tried in secular (non-religious) courts. In Norman England, church courts were introduced to try churchmen separately from lay people.

Page 49 — Norman Church Reform

Knowledge and Understanding

1 The Primacy of Canterbury was a change made by Lanfranc which made the Archbishop of Canterbury the primate of England. This meant the Archbishop of Canterbury was the most important churchman in England, with more power than the Archbishop of York.

2 a) • Lanfranc used councils to impose discipline on the Church.
      • At councils, churchmen discussed different aspects of religious law and made important decisions about how to tackle the Church's problems.

   b) • Church courts were introduced to try churchmen who had been accused of breaking religious law.
      • Church courts gave the Church more control over how churchmen were disciplined.

3 The Normans brought new churchmen to England who were keen on reform, which might have made the process of reform happen more quickly.

4 The Normans popularised the Romanesque style of architecture for religious buildings, bringing England up to date with architectural fashions in Western Europe. This style used features inspired by Roman buildings, such as high arches and wide columns.

5 They believed that supporting the Church was a way of serving God. Building churches also reinforced the Normans' authority, as churches were a permanent, visible symbol of the Normans' dominance over England.

Thinking Historically

1 The Primacy of Canterbury made the position of the Archbishop of Canterbury the most powerful position in the English Church. This made the Church more centralised, which strengthened Lanfranc's control over the Church. This increased authority helped Lanfranc to reform the Church by making it easier for him to tackle corruption and enforce stricter rules for churchmen's behaviour.

2 a) Norman Church reform was important because it helped to enforce discipline on the Church. Lanfranc used councils to impose discipline and enable churchmen to make important decisions about how to deal with the Church's problems. Lanfranc also introduced church courts, giving the Church more control over how churchmen were disciplined. These reforms allowed Lanfranc to improve discipline and enforce stricter rules for how churchmen should behave.

Answers

b) Norman Church reform was important in establishing Norman authority in England. William replaced powerful Anglo-Saxon churchmen, such as archbishops and bishops, with Norman supporters. This helped to increase Norman authority because powerful churchmen were influential figures in society, as they held a lot of land and played an important role in government. As part of their efforts to reform the Church, the Normans also built a lot of new churches, cathedrals and monasteries. These religious buildings helped to reinforce Norman authority as they served as visible and permanent symbols of the Normans' dominance in England.

c) Norman Church reform helped make the Church very wealthy. The Normans granted land to the Church — by 1086, the Church held around a quarter of land in England. This was important because it meant the Church and its senior churchmen had access to a lot of power and wealth.

Page 51 — William I and the Church
Knowledge and Understanding
1 He made large donations to churches and cathedrals and oversaw the construction of new monasteries. He was also very supportive of the idea of reform.

2 • Stigand was too powerful to remove until England was more secure.
• William was able to use Stigand to negotiate with the Anglo-Saxons.

3 a) The Pope was the leader of the Church in Western Europe.
b) The papacy is the office of the Pope.
c) Investiture refers to the appointment of bishops and abbots.

4 Pope Gregory VII wanted to prevent rulers from choosing bishops and abbots because he believed they should be chosen by the Church. However, this caused conflict with rulers in England, France and Germany who wanted to maintain control over the Church in their own countries.

5 William had a good relationship with Pope Alexander II. In 1066, Alexander II supported William's invasion of England and allowed him to march under the Banner of St Peter, a symbol of the Church. In 1070, Alexander's representatives came to England and re-crowned William in a show of support.

6 Pope Gregory VII strongly objected to the Primacy of Canterbury and refused to recognise Lanfranc's increased authority unless he went to Rome and submitted to the Pope. Despite being summoned multiple times, Lanfranc refused to go.

Thinking Historically
1 • He refused to allow the Pope to influence the appointment of bishops and abbots in England. Instead, he appointed churchmen who were loyal to him. This meant they were more likely to support him.
• He reserved the right to overrule important decisions which were made in church councils or courts. This helped him to ensure that he approved of how the Church was being run.
• He took control of communication between England and the Pope. This helped him to control the Pope's influence in England.
• He refused to swear loyalty to the papacy. This limited the Pope's influence in England, which helped William to maintain control of the Church in England.

2 a) The Investiture Controversy caused William's relationship with the Pope to deteriorate. Gregory VII wanted to assert his authority over William, demanding that William should swear loyalty to the papacy and allow the Pope to choose England's bishops and abbots. William resisted Gregory's attempts to assert his authority in England, which led to conflict between William and the Pope.

b) The Investiture Controversy strengthened William's authority in England. The papacy's authority was weakened by the Investiture Controversy, which brought the papacy into conflict with many European rulers such as Henry IV of Germany. This meant the papacy couldn't risk making an enemy of William by forcing him to obey the Pope's demands. William was therefore able to take advantage of the papacy's weakness and refused to let the Pope interfere in England. This strengthened William's authority and his control over England.

Page 53 — William II and the Church
Knowledge and Understanding
1 William had a poor relationship with the Church, which means many sources about him were written by monks who disliked him. As a result, the sources are biased against William, meaning they don't present a balanced view of him.

2 William II made money from the Church by delaying the appointment of senior churchmen and taking the income they would have received for himself.

3 • 1088 — William of Saint-Calais is tried in the king's court for his part in Odo's rebellion and his land is confiscated. The Pope supports William of Saint-Calais and asks for his lands to be restored. William II ignores the Pope. This causes conflict between the Pope and William II.
• 1089 — Archbishop Lanfranc of Canterbury dies. William doesn't appoint a new Archbishop of Canterbury.
• 1093 — After falling seriously ill, William II appoints Anselm as the new Archbishop of Canterbury because William believes God will punish him if dies and the position is still vacant.
• 1095 — At the Council of Rockingham, a group of bishops and nobles tell Anselm to give his ultimate loyalty to the king rather than to the Pope, but Anselm refuses. William II acknowledges Urban II as Pope. In return, Urban agrees not to send representatives or letters to England without William's permission.
• 1097 — William refuses to allow the Church to hold councils, preventing Anselm from making important changes to the Church. Anselm goes to Rome to seek the Pope's support and doesn't return to England until after William's death. Pope Urban II supports Anselm and threatens to excommunicate William II.

4 William of Saint-Calais was the Bishop of Durham, so he wanted to be tried as a churchman in a church court. However, William II insisted the trial take place in the king's court, a decision that was support by other bishops and nobles. This showed that William II had the authority to overrule the Church by trying churchmen in a secular court.

5 The division in the papacy allowed William II to strengthen his own position by not acknowledging either claimant. When he eventually agreed to acknowledge Urban II as Pope, in return Urban agreed not to send representatives or letters to England without the king's permission. This benefited William II as it allowed him to limit the Pope's influence in England.

Answers

Interpretation

1 a) The interpretation convincingly presents the troubled relationship between William and Anselm. The interpretation states that William didn't receive 'the kind of loyalty' he wanted from Anselm. William believed that Anselm's ultimate loyalty should be to the king, but Anselm believed that his loyalty to the Pope was more important. The interpretation is also convincing about the breakdown of William and Anselm's relationship, as it claims that Anselm 'turned to the Pope' for support. This reflects the fact that, after William refused to allow him to hold church councils, Anselm went to Rome to seek the Pope's support and didn't return to England until after William had died.

   b) The interpretation is convincing about William's relationship with English bishops. The interpretation states that the leading English bishops wanted Anselm to 'pledge himself wholly' to the king, suggesting they supported William. This is convincing because it reflects the bishops' loyalty to William at the Council of Rockingham in 1095, where they told Anselm to obey the king.

   c) The interpretation is convincing about William's poor relationship with the Pope. The interpretation states that the Pope 'threatened William', suggesting that the pair had a difficult relationship and came into conflict with each other. This is convincing because it reflects the fact that Urban II threatened William with excommunication after William prevented Anselm from holding church councils in 1097.

Page 55 — Norman Monasticism

Knowledge and Understanding

1 There were many abbeys and monasteries in England before the conquest. They were wealthy and powerful because kings and the nobility supported them with valuable gifts and land. All Anglo-Saxon monks followed the Rule of St Benedict, but monasteries interpreted the Rule differently and operated differently as a result.

2 Many Anglo-Saxon monasteries were damaged by the conquest. They were an easy target for the Normans who took their land and wealth. Some of this land was given to monasteries in Normandy, but most of it was claimed by secular lords.

3 a) It was founded by William I on the site of the Battle of Hastings, possibly as a symbol of William's victory over Harold.

   b) It was built in 1083 by the Norman Earl of Shrewsbury, Roger of Montgomery, on the site of an Anglo-Saxon church.

   c) It was one of many abbeys and monasteries that had been abandoned in northern England between the 8th and 10th centuries due to Viking raids. The Normans refounded some of these abbeys and monasteries, including Whitby in about 1078.

4 The Normans were worried that God would punish them for the violence of the conquest and thought that building monasteries would help them to earn forgiveness.

5 a) The Cluniacs were a group of monks from the Abbey of Cluny in France. In the 11th century, they started to reform and reorganise monasteries across Europe and wanted monks to follow the Rule of St Benedict more strictly. The Cluniacs' ideas were brought to England by the Normans after the conquest, and Cluniac monks arrived in England in the late 1070s. By 1100, there were lots of Cluniac monasteries in England.

   b) The Augustinians were a groups of monks who followed the Rule of St Augustine instead of the Rule of St Benedict, which meant they lived a different lifestyle to the Benedictines. They arrived in England after the Cluniacs, founding monasteries at Canterbury, Colchester and Huntingdon in the 1090s.

Thinking Historically

1 a) William I replaced most Anglo-Saxon abbots with Normans, including at monasteries in Peterborough, Glastonbury and Winchester.

   b) The Normans didn't get rid of Anglo-Saxon monks, but a lot of monks came from Normandy, especially to join new monasteries. Different types of monks, such as Cluniacs and Augustinians, also came over to England as a result of the conquest.

   c) New groups of monks came to England after the conquest and many of them had different ideas about the Rule that monks should follow. For example, the Cluniacs followed the Rule of St Benedict, but more strictly than Anglo-Saxon monks, and the Augustinians followed the Rule of St Augustine.

   d) The Normans were very open to monastic reform. Monasteries in Normandy had been affected by the Cluniacs' reforms and the Normans brought these ideas to England after the conquest. The new abbots and monks who came to England were probably more open to reform than Anglo-Saxon abbots and monks. These changes encouraged reform to take place in English monasteries.

Page 57 — Life in a Norman Monastery

Knowledge and Understanding

1 It was meant to keep them away from the distractions of ordinary life and help them to devote their lives to God.

2 a) Monks woke up early in the morning, at around two o'clock, for the first service of the day and had their final service of the day at around seven o'clock in the evening. Monks attended eight services a day, which were often performed in Latin. During the services, monks prayed and sang or chanted religious songs.

   b) Between services, the monks did tasks that were essential to the running of the monastery, such as managing supplies. They also spent a lot of time reading and writing.

   c) Monks ate two meals a day, and weren't allowed to eat meat as it was a luxury.

3 Abbots were influential figures in society — they were major landholders and owed service to the king. Ordinary monks helped poorer people in the local area by giving food to those who were hungry and medical care to those who were ill. They also played an important role in education and contributed to culture with works of art, literature and music. Monks also provided accommodation for pilgrims who visited their monasteries.

Thinking Historically

1 a) Change — Anglo-Saxon monasteries varied in layout and often had multiple churches, whereas most Norman monasteries were built with a standard layout and only had a single church. Norman monasteries usually had a cloister attached to their church, but cloisters weren't a regular feature in Anglo-Saxon monasteries.

   b) Change — The content of services changed after the conquest, as the Normans introduced new practices.

   c) Continuity — Many of the saints that people worshipped stayed the same. Although the Normans had different traditions, they kept existing saints in an attempt to keep the Anglo-Saxons satisfied.

Answers

Interpretation

1 a) The large windows are convincing because cloisters in monasteries were often designed to allow sunlight in, so may have had large windows to allow this to happen.

b) The stone pillars are convincing because the Normans usually built monastic buildings from stone, whereas the Anglo-Saxons often used wood.

c) The fact that there are only monks and no lay people is convincing because Norman monasteries allowed monks to live away from lay people. Monks lived separately from other people so they could devote their lives to God.

d) This is convincing because monks often used the cloister in a monastery as a scriptorium, a place where they could read or write.

Page 59 — Education and Literacy

Knowledge and Understanding

1 Books were written by scribes (monks who were able to write). Scribes spent their time creating copies of existing texts and writing new texts. Monks had to prepare all the materials they needed to produce the books, such as ink and parchment. They also illustrated many of their books with bright colours or decorated them with gold.

2 The vernacular is the language used by ordinary people in a particular area.

Interpretation

1 a) The interpretation is convincing because it shows a monk educating a pupil. Most people who were educated in Norman England were taught by monks in monastic schools.

b) The interpretation is convincing because it shows a young boy being taught. Most pupils in Norman England were boys who were sent to monasteries at a young age and brought up to become monks, though some pupils became government officials. However, the interpretation doesn't reflect the fact that a small number of girls received an education from nuns.

c) The interpretation is convincing because it presents a pupil writing as the monk directs him, and writing was one of the key skills taught at monastic schools. The image also presents the monk holding a book towards the pupil, reflecting the fact that reading was another important skill pupils were taught.

Thinking Historically

1 a) Before 1066, people in England spoke Old English. After 1066, Old English changed to include French words.

b) Norman settlers in England spoke Old French and introduced French loanwords into English.

c) Before the conquest, the main written language was Old English. After the conquest, Latin became the dominant language for written texts.

d) At first, royal documents were issued in English. William then introduced bilingual documents that were written in both Old English and Latin so they could be understood by Anglo-Saxons and Normans. He issued governments documents almost exclusively in Latin after 1070.

Page 61 — Exam-Style Questions

1 This question is level marked. You should look at the level descriptions on page 62 to help you mark your answer. Here are some points your answer may include:

- The interpretation is convincing because it presents William I's uneasy relationship with the papacy. The interpretation states that the relationship was 'not a comfortable one'. This refers to the conflict between William and Pope Gregory VII that was caused by Gregory trying to assert the papacy's authority over William. Gregory wanted the Church to appoint England's bishops and abbots, and wanted William to swear loyalty to the papacy. However, William resisted, refusing to swear loyalty or allow the Pope to appoint bishops and abbots in England. This led to the deterioration of William's relationship with the papacy.

- The interpretation is convincing because it presents William as one of many rulers who had a difficult relationship with the papacy. The interpretation says that William was 'not alone' in coming into conflict with Gregory VII and that other European rulers also clashed with the Pope. Gregory VII came into conflict with rulers in France and Germany during the Investiture Controversy, as the papacy wanted to appoint bishops and abbots but the rulers wanted to maintain control over the Church in their own countries. Disagreements over this issue led to Henry IV of Germany attempting to remove Gregory VII as Pope in 1080.

- The interpretation convincingly shows that William managed to benefit from his relationship with the papacy. The interpretation states that William was able to take advantage of the papacy's 'weakness'. The papacy was weakened during the Investiture Controversy, which brought it into conflict with a number of European rulers. This meant that, although Gregory VII wanted to assert authority over William, he couldn't afford to make a serious enemy of William. This enabled William to create 'compromises' with the Pope, such as agreeing to pay Peter's Pence but refusing to swear loyalty to him.

- The interpretation is not entirely convincing, as it doesn't consider the positive relationship William had with the papacy before 1073. The interpretation says that for 'much of his reign' William did not have a good relationship with the papacy. However, Pope Alexander II supported William's invasion of England in 1066 and allowed him to march under the Banner of St Peter, a symbol of the Church. The Pope's representatives also came to England to re-crown William in another show of support in 1070. This shows that William's relationship with the papacy was more comfortable in the first few years of his reign.

2   This question is level marked. You should look at the level descriptions on page 62 to help you mark your answer. Here are some points your answer may include:
- The appointment of Lanfranc as Archbishop of Canterbury was important because it helped the Normans to maintain control of England. Replacing the existing Anglo-Saxon Archbishop, Stigand, with Lanfranc gave William a loyal supporter in one of the most powerful positions in the Church. It was important for William to have the Church's support, as churchmen held a lot of land and played an important role in government. The Church's support could also help to legitimise William's claim to the throne, as it suggested that God also supported him. Lanfranc's appointment as Archbishop of Canterbury helped to strengthen Norman control over the Church and ensure that the Church supported William's rule.
- The appointment of Archbishop Lanfranc was important because Lanfranc changed the structure of the Church. He established the Primacy of Canterbury, which made the Archbishop of Canterbury the most powerful figure in the English Church. This made the Church more centralised, strengthening Lanfranc's control over the Church. Changing the structure of the Church made it made it easier for Lanfranc to impose changes and reform the English Church.
- Lanfranc's appointment was important because he encouraged reform in the English Church. Before coming to England, he was an abbot in Normandy and had been influenced by the movement for Church reform that was spreading through Europe. When he became Archbishop of Canterbury, he wanted to tackle corruption in the English Church, such as the problems of simony, nepotism, pluralism and clerical marriage. Lanfranc used councils to tackle corruption by imposing discipline on the Church and enabling churchmen to discuss how to deal with the Church's problems. Lanfranc's appointment and his efforts to tackle corruption may have helped to speed up the rate of Church reform in England.
- Lanfranc's appointment was important because he made changes to the justice system in England. Before Lanfranc was appointed, churchmen were tried in secular courts. However, Lanfranc introduced Church courts to England, meaning that churchmen could be tried with less secular interference. This gave the Church greater control over disciplining churchmen who broke religious laws.
- Lanfranc's appointment as Archbishop of Canterbury was important because it contributed to England's difficult relationship with the papacy. Pope Gregory VII objected to the Primacy of Canterbury and refused to recognise Lanfranc's increased authority unless he went to Rome and submitted to the Pope. However, Lanfranc refused to go. This tension between Lanfranc and the Pope worsened the relationship between England and the papacy, which was already strained because William was resisting Gregory's attempts to assert his authority in England.

3   This question is level marked. You should look at the level descriptions on page 62 to help you mark your answer. Here are some points your answer may include:
- Initially, monasteries in England were damaged by the conquest. Before 1066, Anglo-Saxon monasteries were very wealthy as they were given valuable gifts and land by kings and the nobility. However, the Normans took land and wealth from the monasteries after the conquest. Some of the land was given to monasteries in Normandy, but the majority of it was claimed by secular lords. The loss of land and wealth had a devastating impact on monasticism in England.
- An important change to monasticism was that the Normans helped to revive monastic life after the conquest. The king and members of the nobility built new abbeys and monasteries in England. For example, William I founded Battle Abbey on the site of the Battle of Hastings, and Roger of Montgomery, Earl of Shrewsbury, founded Shrewsbury Abbey. The Normans also refounded abbeys and monasteries in northern England that had been abandoned due to Viking raids between the 8th and 10th centuries, such as Whitby Abbey. The building of so many abbeys and monasteries helped monastic life in England to recover from the initial destruction of the conquest.
- The Normans encouraged monastic reform after the conquest. Before 1066, Anglo-Saxon monks all followed the Rule of St Benedict, but monasteries interpreted the Rule differently and as a result operated differently. Many monasteries in Normandy had been influenced by the Cluniacs, who wanted to reform monasticism and ensure that monks followed the Rule of St Benedict more strictly. After the conquest, Norman monks brought the Cluniacs' ideas to monasteries in England. Abbots also influenced reform in England, as William appointed Norman abbots to replace Anglo-Saxons ones in monasteries such as Peterborough, Glastonbury and Winchester. These new abbots often held different beliefs from the old ones, so their appointments may have led to reforms in their monasteries after the conquest.
- Monasticism changed after the conquest because different types of monks came to England and founded monasteries. The Cluniacs arrived in England in the late 1070s, and William de Warenne founded a Cluniac monastery at Lewes soon after. The Cluniacs followed the Rule of St Benedict more strictly than the Anglo-Saxon monks did, so their arrival brought changes to monastic life in England. Augustinians also arrived in England, and Augustinian monasteries were founded at Canterbury, Colchester and Huntingdon in the 1090s. The Augustinians lived a different lifestyle from the Benedictines, so the Augustinians' arrival brought more variety to monasticism in England, as all English monks before the conquest had been Benedictines.

Index

HANEO41